SHOGUN

The life of Lord Tokugawa Ieyasu

This catalogue illustrates all the objects from the exhibition *Shogun: The Life of Lord Tokugawa Ieyasu*, held at the Royal Armouries Museum, Leeds from 6 June – 30 August 2005, produced in association with Nikko Toshogu Shrine.

For reasons of conservation not all objects are on display for the duration of the exhibition. Some objects will be changed between 18 – 20 July 2005.

Exhibition curator: Ian Bottomley
Exhibition designer: Graham Moores
Exhibition design assistants: Geraldine Mead, Darren Snaith
Technicians: Alan Eyles, Jonathan Morris, Andy Todd
Conservation: Suzanne Kitto, Fiona Cahill, Emma Schmuecker
Registrars: Caroline Rhodes, Katherine Richmond
Project coordinator: Karen Whitting

With thanks to all the staff of Royal Armouries Museum for their contributions and support in the staging of this exhibition.

Catalogue author: Ian Bottomley
Contributors: Peter Armstrong, Adrian Budge, Claire Harder, Hoshino Fujio, Thom Richardson, Graeme Rimer, Inaba Takamasa, Shibata Yoshitaka
Catalogue designer: Geraldine Mead
Editor: Debbie Wurr
Royal Armouries photography: Rod Joyce

Royal Armouries Museum
Armouries Drive
Leeds, LS10 1LT

ISBN 0 948092 58 0

Printed in Great Britain by BAS Printers Limited

Throughout the catalogue the Japanese convention of placing the family name first when referring to an individual has been used, for example: Matsudaira Hirotada.

Front cover and half-title page: Portrait of Lord Tokugawa Ieyasu by Kobori Tomoto, about 1930. Nikko Toshogu Shrine

Title page: Portrait of Lord Tokugawa Ieyasu by Kano Ryotaku, early 17th century. Nikko Toshogu Shrine

ROYAL
ARMOURIES

The Royal Armouries would like to thank the following sponsors for their significant contributions to the success of the exhibition:

Supported by

YORKSHIRE FORWARD

JAL

JAPAN AIRLINES

JAPAN'S LEADING AIRLINE

Pioneer

sound. vision. soul

Technical partner for Shogun

大和日英基金

The Daiwa Anglo-Japanese Foundation

The Royal Armouries would also like to thank the following organisations for their support:

JAPANFOUNDATION

EUROPEAN UNION JAPAN 2005

The Embassy of Japan in the United Kingdom

The Ministry of Japanese Cultural Affairs

The GB Sasakawa Foundation

Leeds Philosophical and Literary Society

Above: Tokugawa Ieyasu's mother praying.

Images on pages 6, 10 – 11, 13, 15, 17, 18 – 19, 22 – 27 and 32 are taken from the scrolls on the founding of Nikko, by Kano Tanyu, about 1640.

CONTENTS

NIKKO TOSHOGU SHRINE

Greetings from Nikko Toshogu Shrine

Fourteen years have now passed since 1991, when the Royal Armouries was twinned with Nikko Toshogu. The intervening years have seen the partnership between our two establishments steadily strengthened through a succession of exchange programmes, including mutual-exchange exhibitions of treasures, demonstrations in the UK of traditional Japanese horseback archery as performed annually at our shrine, and performances in Nikko by a British medieval martial arts group.

It gives me great pleasure that these exchange programmes are now about to bear fruit in our long-planned co-hosting of the special exhibition *Shogun: The Life of Lord Tokugawa Ieyasu.*

Born in the strife-torn period of Japan's civil war, Lord Tokugawa Ieyasu, to whom our shrine is dedicated, was the great statesman who laid the foundations of modern Japan. Overcoming all sorts of adversity, he succeeded in unifying the country, and ushered in the Edo era, a 260-year period of peace unparalleled in world history. Here at Nikko Toshogu, we hope that this exhibition will be seen by large numbers of visitors from the UK and other countries, increasing public awareness of his extraordinary achievements.

Finally, I would like to express heartfelt thanks to the entire staff of the Royal Armouries, Leeds, who have given us special assistance with regard to the exhibits.

稲葉久雄

Hisao Inaba
Head Priest, Nikko Toshogu Shrine

2301 Sannai Nikko, Tochigi
Telephone: 0288-54-0560

ROYAL
ARMOURIES

Armouries Drive
Leeds
Yorkshire LS10 1LT
Telephone 0113 220 1999

I am delighted to be able to welcome you to the Royal Armouries and this remarkable exhibition – *Shogun: The Life of Lord Tokugawa Ieyasu.*

This unprecedented event is the culmination of a 14-year partnership between the Royal Armouries and the world heritage site, the Nikko Toshogu Shrine in Japan. In fact, this strong connection between the two countries and cultures can be traced back still further to over 400 years ago when the Tokugawa Shogun gave King James I a gift of a suit of armour. This armour is just one of the stunning objects on display in our ground-breaking exhibition.

It is a great honour for the Royal Armouries to be entrusted with these sacred objects, which are being brought together for the first time outside of Japan. This project has been a major investment of time and energy, whose success has depended on the knowledge, skill, enthusiasm and hard work of a large number of institutions and individuals both in the UK and in Japan. Although there are too many names to be acknowledged here, special thanks go to Mr Hisao Inaba, Head Priest of the Nikko Shrine. Without Mr Inaba's personal commitment and the support of all the Toshogu shrines, this exhibition would not have taken place.

This event is an example of the Royal Armouries' ongoing commitment to bring objects and stories from across the world to life, for the enjoyment and education of everyone. I hope that you enjoy the exhibition and the activities around it and that this catalogue is something you will keep to bring back memories of this extraordinary exhibition and the story of Tokugawa Ieyasu, Japan's most famous Shogun.

Ann M Green
Chairman, Royal Armouries

Above: Tokugawa Ieyasu's mother has a divinely inspired dream.

Above right: The birth of Tokugawa Ieyasu. The archer on the veranda drives away evil spirits.

POLITICAL & SOCIAL BACKGROUND

The following essay is not intended to be a comprehensive biography of Lord Tokugawa Ieyasu, but an outline of some of the military exploits that led him to the pivotal battle of Seki ga Hara and beyond.

Late in the year 1542 an event took place that was to have a momentous impact on Japanese history; a son was born to a nobleman named Matsudaira Hirotada, Lord of the province of Mikawa.

Just a half a year later another significant event occurred on the island of Tanegashima off the southern tip of Kyushu. On 25 August 1543 on board a Chinese vessel seeking shelter from a violent storm were three Portuguese traders, who carried guns. The Japan into which Matsudaira Hirotada's son was born, on 26 December 1542, and in which the three Portuguese found themselves, was one torn by civil wars. Internal wars had been common enough throughout Japanese history, but the civil wars that were then raging were exceptional. Territorial lords, the *daimyo* ('great names'), had been fighting each other for land, and for the power it brought, for almost a century. Constantly shifting patterns of alliances were formed and reformed to take advantage of every changing circumstance, yet nobody had achieved the ultimate prize of creating a sufficiently large power base to take overall control. Unlike the nobility, who had dominated warfare in the past, the *daimyo* fighting these civil wars were perfectly happy to recruit farmers and peasants to swell the ranks of their armies. Firearms, brought by the Portuguese, introduced a new factor into the equation.

The arrival of the gun

Literary references indicate that a gun of some kind had been introduced from China decades earlier, and that it had been copied and used by the Japanese, but whatever it was it failed to make any significant impression. In contrast, the gun introduced by the Portuguese, almost certainly of the type being produced in their base in Goa, India, was recognized by a few farsighted *daimyo* as being of immense value. It was true that an archer could shoot about as far as these guns, and could loose off about a dozen arrows in the time it took to reload the gun, but he needed years of training. A gun in the hands of a common soldier, with only a few days practice, made him an effective adversary of the most highly trained warrior. It did however require a complete revision of military thinking. These new and expensive weapons were given to the lowest ranking troops and warriors, skilled in the more traditional weapons of bow and sword, had to take a supporting role.

Within a very few years gun production had become a major industry in towns such as Sakai and Kunimoto as orders were placed to equip the armies. Only six years after their introduction, a noble called Oda Nobuhide (+ 1549) was able to place an order for 500 guns in Kunimoto. Twenty years later, armies equipped with thousands of guns were commonplace. It has been estimated that by 1600 there were still some 200,000 guns in Japan. During the second half of the 16th century Japan was the world's largest manufacturer and user of guns.

In the wake of these first Portuguese traders came priests of the Society of Jesus, eager to gain converts to Christianity. It did not take the Portuguese long to appreciate that the diplomatic tensions that then existed between Japan and Ming China could be turned to their advantage. Raw silk and Chinese brocades were in great demand in Japan, a demand that was only partially met by pirate traders. Soon Portuguese ships were sailing from their base in Goa, carrying goods such as textiles, ivory and wine to trade with the Chinese in Macao. There they loaded the raw silk, brocades and similar luxury goods for sale in Japan, returning to Goa with silver and items for shipment onwards to Europe.

The arrival of the Portuguese, and the introduction of the gun had little immediate effect on most of the *daimyo,* who continued fighting for power and land. Lord Matsudaira Hirotada's province of Mikawa was bordered by two powerful neighbours, one being the above-mentioned gun-buying Oda Nobuhide and the other Imagawa Yoshimoto (1519–60). In 1547 Matsudaira Hirotada's uncle, Matsudaira Nobutaka, attacked him in a struggle for the leadership of the Matsudaira, prompting Matsudaira Hirotada to approach the Imagawa to form a coalition.

Tokugawa Ieyasu's rise to power

One of the conditions of the coalition, a perfectly normal demand at the time, was that Lord Matsudaira Hirotada should send his young son, whom he had called Matsudaira Takechiyo, to stay with the Imagawa in their capital at Sumpu as a hostage. Unfortunately for the alliance, and for the young child, news of the transfer leaked out and the party was ambushed by Oda forces and spirited away to their castle at Kowatari in Owari. Despite Oda Nobuhide's threats to murder the child, Matsudaira Hirotada, to his credit, ignored the threats and refused to break his agreement with the Imagawa. Seizing the opportunity Imagawa Yoshimoto dispatched an army to the Oda fort at Anjo and captured Oda Nobuhide's son, who was lord of the castle. Then Imagawa Yoshimoto negotiated an exchange of prisoners, and thus rather than attacking he agreed to withdraw if the young Matsudaira Takechiyo was handed over. Thus the child finally reached Sumpu after a delay of nearly a year. Once established in his new home he was afforded the comforts of an honoured guest, he was given an education and lived in a style befitting a young Japanese noble of the time.

On coming of age in 1555 Matsudaira Takechiyo took the adult name of Matsudaira Nobumoto and later still changed it to Matsudaira Motoyasu; the character 'Moto' being bestowed upon him by Imagawa Yoshimoto himself and the 'Yasu' from his grandfather Kiyoyasu. With his father dead he was now head of the Matsudaira family. Matsudaira Motoyasu and his men were expected to fight as allies alongside the Imagawa army. In 1558 Imagawa Yoshimoto tested the 17-year-old Matsudaira Motoyasu in action for the first time. He was asked to attack a castle held by Suzuki Shigetatsu, who had defected from the Imagawa to the Oda. To avoid depleting his forces Matsudaira Motoyasu simply fired the castle. Within a few days he had defeated four other forts and had gained a countrywide reputation.

Inevitably Matsudaira Motoyasu came up against Oda Nobunaga (1534–82), the second son of Oda Nobuhide, who had taken control of Owari after his father's death against considerable opposition from his relatives. He even fought a battle against his younger brother, eventually ordering him to commit suicide.

The encounter with the Matsudaira occurred because Oda Nobunaga was laying siege to a minor outpost that was rapidly running out of supplies. It fell to Matsudaira Motoyasu to re-supply the beleaguered garrison. As young as he was, he could see that a direct attack on the Oda army would have been a futile gesture. Instead he sent out false intelligence that tricked Oda Nobunaga into dispatching the bulk of his force to counter a non-existent attack, supposedly approaching from a different direction. As soon as Oda Nobunaga and the majority of his troops had left the fortress, the Matsudaira forces swept in and relieved the garrison of Odaka virtually unopposed.

Although these attempts by the Oda to encroach onto the Matsudaira and Imagawa lands needed careful monitoring and swift action, to Imagawa Yoshimoto they were simply a distraction. He had set his sights on a far higher goal. By 1560 he had assembled an army of some 20,000, including the Matsudaira men, with which he hoped to support the emperor in Kyoto, the imperial capital and the location of the court of the shogun.

The origins of the civil wars

Japan has had an unbroken line of emperors for well over a thousand years but for much of this time the real government of the country was in the hands of military rulers. At the head of this alternative government was the shogun, or more properly *Seii Taishogun,* 'Barbarian-destroying Great General'; a title with its origins in Japan's ancient past. The first of these military rulers was Minamoto Yoritomo who, in the 12th century, led his clan in the defeat of their military rivals and was granted permission to rule by the emperor. Minamoto Yoritomo is also one of the gods of the Nikko Toshogu Shrine because he is an ancestor of the Tokugawa family. He set up his military government, called the *bakufu,* in Kamakura and delegated the administration of the provinces to land stewards called *jito* and constables called *shugo.* By the mid 14th century the shogunate was in the hands of the Ashikaga family and under their rule the power of the shogunate grew until they controlled virtually all military and political affairs. Similarly the *shugo* also expanded their roles until they had become, in effect, the military governors of the provinces. Subsequent generations of Ashikaga shoguns gradually lost much of their power, preferring to indulge themselves in the pleasurable life of the imperial capital rather than managing the affairs of state. Similarly many of the *shugo* found life in Kyoto far more amenable than a rustic existence in some rural backwater. They preferred to appoint deputies called *kokujin* to reside in the various territories and manage them on their behalf.

Above right: The 10-year-old Tokugawa Ieyasu carried on the back of a retainer watches a mock battle on the bank of a river.

It had been *shugo* who had been partly responsible for the civil wars. In 1467 a dispute had arisen between rival *shugo* that led to a protracted urban war fought almost entirely within the city of Kyoto. By the time the conflict petered out, some ten years later, these urban *shugo*, their armies depleted and exhausted, were in a parlous state. Their placemen around the country, who had governed their fiefs without interference for ten years, resented all attempts to re-impose control from the centre, and were quite prepared to fight for what they held. Noble families, who had been in power for centuries, suffered defeat and extermination when they tried to reclaim their holdings. It was the beginning of an era that is now known as the *Senkoku Jidai* or the 'age of the country at war', one consequence of which was the phenomenon of *gekokujo* or the overthrow of the traditional nobility by those of lower rank.

It was this weakened central authority that Imagawa Yoshimoto had hopes of reinforcing. Hardly had his army of 20,000 left their base and headed towards Kyoto, when Matsudaira Motoyasu and a small contingent of Matsudaira soldiers were detached from the main column to attack a minor fort called Marune. Although the defenders put up considerable resistance, the fort was eventually taken. While Matsudaira Motoyasu was occupied with this task, Oda forces swept down on the main Imagawa army at Okehazama, decimating it and killing Imagawa Yoshimoto in the process.

With the Imagawa now a spent force, Matsudaira Motoyasu retreated to Mikawa where he sensibly entrenched for a while, allowing the Matsudaira fortunes to build up and giving his war-torn province an opportunity to recover. In 1566 he petitioned Kyoto to allow him to change his family name from Matsudaira to Tokugawa, that being the name of the area that his family originated from. He also set down his family's pedigree, tracing it back to the Nitta clan and through them to Minamoto Yoritomo who had first held the title of shogun. At the same time he changed his personal name finally settling on Ieyasu, the name by which he is known to history. He was now known as Tokugawa Ieyasu, Lord of the province of Mikawa.

The alliance of Tokugawa Ieyasu and Oda Nobunaga

In 1567, with his new name and his armies refreshed, Tokugawa Ieyasu now sought an alliance with Oda Nobunaga. When Oda Nobunaga decided to march on Kyoto in 1568, Tokugawa Ieyasu and his men joined him in the venture. Being allied to the Oda did not however inhibit Tokugawa Ieyasu from sounding out other potential allies. One such was Takeda Shingen (1521 – 73), Lord of Kai and Shinano provinces. Takeda Shingen was a commander who was renowned for the size and effectiveness of his army, particularly his cavalry, as well as the efficiency of the administrative system that supported it. He placed great faith in the Chinese military classics and had as his standard a flag with the characters *fu* (wind), *rin* (forest), *ka* (fire) and *zan* (mountain) on it; interpreted as 'move as fast as the wind, as silently as the forest, strike like fire and be as steady as a mountain'. Had Takeda Shingen not spent much of his time fighting his neighbour and fellow Buddhist, Uesugi Kenshin, he may have made an even greater mark on Japanese history. In 1568 Tokugawa Ieyasu and Takeda Shingen together conquered and divided up the old Imagawa territories. Having acquired this new land, Tokugawa Ieyasu moved his base from his old capital at Okazaki in Mikawa to the castle of Hamamatsu, situated on the Tokaido road that connected Kyoto to the North.

In 1568, while Tokugawa Ieyasu and Takeda Shingen were busy in the old Imagawa lands, Oda Nobunaga had gained control of Kyoto and had made his own man, Ashikaga Yoshiaki, shogun. He now turned his attention northwards but found his route threatened by the military monks based in the Buddhist temple of Enryakuji on Mount Hiei. These and other monasteries had been a significant military and political threat for centuries as a result of a piece of ill-conceived legislation that had granted tax-free status to the land they owned. Imaginative monks had devised a profitable tax-mitigation scheme whereby, for a fee, the owners of land could nominally sign over title to the monks and receive the income from it tax-free. To protect these holdings, and other business ventures, many monasteries maintained considerable armies, the warriors being only thinly disguised as novices. Oda Nobunaga had little regard for religion and a positive dislike of the more militant Buddhists. On 12 September 1571, showing his usual ruthlessness, Oda Nobunaga had Mount Hiei surrounded by his troops who, at a signal, climbed the pathways to the summit, burning the buildings and killing everyone they encountered.

In December 1572 Oda Nobunaga's move northward and Tokugawa Ieyasu's relocation to Hamamatsu was interpreted by Takeda Shingen as being distinctly provocative. In a pre-emptive move he marched his army of 35,000 men by a circuitous route towards Hamamatsu. Word of this manoeuvre soon reached Oda Nobunaga who dispatched reinforcements to Tokugawa Ieyasu with the suggestion that he exhibit caution. Tokugawa Ieyasu, although considerably outnumbered, insisted on leaving his stronghold and facing Takeda Shingen a few miles to the north of Hamamatsu Castle at Mikata ga Hara. Late in the afternoon the two armies met and the fighting continued until long after nightfall. Despite the bravery of the Tokugawa army, Takeda Shingen's superior forces gradually gained the upper hand. Tokugawa Ieyasu, who had narrowly escaped death at least twice during the fighting, finally gave the order to withdraw back to Hamamatsu. He then did something totally unexpected. Rather than shutting the gates of Hamamatsu, Tokugawa Ieyasu ordered them left open and ordered fires to be lit to guide the stragglers in. This ruse took Takeda Shingen entirely by surprise and caused him to hesitate. The signs indicated that there were far more defenders inside than he had estimated. Instead of driving home his advantage, he chose caution and withdrew to review the situation in daylight. During the early hours of the following morning, a small band of Tokugawa men quietly left the castle and harried the Takeda forces in their camp, an action that only compounded Takeda Shingen's uncertainties. With the weather closing in and winter coming on, Takeda Shingen decided to withdraw back to his mountain provinces and leave Tokugawa Ieyasu for a later date.

Takeda Shingen died the following year leaving his army to his ambitious but rather impetuous son Takeda Katsuyori (1546–82). By May 1575 Takeda Katsuyori felt that he was ready to deal with his father's unfinished business and laid siege to one of Tokugawa Ieyasu's castles at Nagashino in Mikawa. Once again Tokugawa Ieyasu and Oda Nobunaga combined their forces and assembled an army of about 38,000 men to relieve the garrison. Takeda Katsuyori had no intention of fighting near the castle, moving his troops some distance away to a more open location that would allow him to exploit his famous cavalry. The allies anticipated this strategy and built palisades to protect their 3,000 or so musket-armed soldiers, siting them not far from a stream that they reasoned would slow the horses. This tactic proved decisive as wave after wave of Takeda forces were gunned down as they slowed to negotiate the ditch. The once mighty Takeda army was decimated by the intelligent use of volley fire. Takeda Katsuyori himself managed to escape with the remnants of his forces and retreated to his mountainous homelands to recover.

By May 1582 Tokugawa Ieyasu and Oda Nobunaga had jointly annihilated the remnants of the Takeda army and Tokugawa Ieyasu added the former Takeda province of Suruga to his domain. Together the two allies had conquered, and were occupying, a considerable portion of Japan. This successful partnership was abruptly terminated by the assassination of Oda Nobunaga in Kyoto by another of his supposed supporters, Akechi Mitsuhide. One of Oda Nobunaga's most able generals, Hashiba Hideyoshi (1536–98), a peasant who had risen by his abilities, rallied his troops and rushed to Kyoto to avenge his lord.

Japanese visit Europe

Whilst Tokugawa Ieyasu and Oda Nobunaga were making their mark on Honshu, the main island of Japan, trade with the Portuguese had continued unabated in Kyushu. All was not well however with the Europeans in the East. In 1580 an event in Europe caused them considerable consternation. King Philip II of Spain had moved into Lisbon and had taken the vacant throne of Portugal. With Philip in control of the whole Iberian Peninsula there was a very real fear amongst the Portuguese in the East that he would favour the Spanish and allow them to take over control of the Portuguese operations. In a move to forestall him, four Japanese youths from the Arima, Omura and Otomo families, all baptized Christians, journeyed to Europe in 1582 to demonstrate to the devoutly catholic king how successful the Jesuits had been in spreading the Christian faith in Japan. Hashiba Hideyoshi learned of this expedition and recognized its importance to the maintenance of the silk trade. To this end he sent

Above right: Tokugawa Ieyasu leads his troops at the battle of Nagakute.

personal gifts for King Philip II that included weapons and armours, in Japanese eyes the only proper gifts between statesmen.

The alliance of Tokugawa Ieyasu and Toyotomi Hideyashi

After catching and defeating Akechi Mitsudehide, Hashiba Hideyoshi took command of the former Oda army, an action that Tokugawa Ieyasu viewed as an outrage. He felt that command of the Oda forces should properly have passed to Oda Nobukatsu, one of Oda Nobunaga's sons. In response to this takeover, Tokugawa Ieyasu sent an army into Owari in 1584 to make a stand against Hashiba Hideyoshi at Komaki. There followed a series of actions that culminated in the battle of Nagakute in 1584. Although there were losses on both sides, it was a campaign in which neither side could be said to have gained any real advantage. Having experienced Hashiba Hideyoshi's ability to command an army at first hand, Tokugawa Ieyasu wisely reached the conclusion that it would be better to join Hashiba Hideyoshi than oppose him. In an act of conciliation, Tokugawa Ieyasu arrived the following spring at Osaka Castle, Hashiba Hideyoshi's stronghold, to make peace. Not unnaturally, Hashiba Hideyoshi was deeply suspicious and, although courteous, declined Tokugawa Ieyasu's offer to assist in his campaign to conquer the islands of Shikoku and Kyushu.

By 1585 Hashiba Hideyoshi had gained control of a large part of the country but was unable to receive the title of shogun because of his lowly birth. Instead he was granted the title *Kampaku,* implying 'one who assists the emperor'. He was also given the name Toyotomi, meaning 'prosperous subject of the emperor', the name by which he is known to history. It was not until Toyotomi Hideyoshi turned his attention northwards to the Kanto region that he called on Tokugawa Ieyasu and his troops to join with his armies. In 1590 the combined forces of Toyotomi Hideyoshi and Tokugawa Ieyasu moved northwards to take the province of Odawara from the powerful Hojo family.

The illustrious and ancient name of Hojo had been adopted by a warrior family, one which had acquired territory through aggression and treachery, to give themselves at least a superficial appearance of respectability. The Hojo stronghold, garrisoned by some 56,000 defenders, was besieged for three months by the combined force of Toyotomi Hideyoshi and Tokugawa Ieyasu numbering some 200,000 men. Eventually, by mining and aided by a violent storm, a breach was finally created that could be exploited, and the Hojo capitulated. Toyotomi Hideyoshi suggested to Tokugawa Ieyasu that he might exchange the eight Hojo provinces situated in the fertile Kanto plain for his five mountainous provinces. As a result, in August 1590, Tokugawa Ieyasu moved out of Mikawa, Totomi, Suruga, Shinano and Kai. He was now immensely wealthy; the lord of the fertile Kanto plains with an income of around 1,000,000 *koku* of rice per annum (one *koku* being approximately the amount of rice needed to feed a man for a year). He set up his new headquarters in a small fishing village that was later to become the city of Edo and eventually Tokyo.

Although there was now peace, *Kampaku* Toyotomi Hideyoshi was faced with the problem of trying to maintain it in a country that contained a vast number of armed men who had known no other life but fighting. Traditionally, loyal allies and vassals had been given grants of land for their military service, but land was now scarce. Instead Toyotomi Hideyoshi instituted the practice of giving fine swords as rewards, as well as introducing a series of reforms to minimise the threat of insurrection. He reformed the taxation of rice production and established a survey that established who had the right to bear arms. Tenants, who in the past had put on their armour and marched off to join their lord in battle, were forced to make the choice of becoming an armed retainer or living the simple life of the farmer. Inspectors were appointed to tour the provinces confiscating weapons from all but those who could show they were of military class.

Toyotomi Hideyoshi's invasions of Korea

There was also a growing problem, particularly in Kyushu, that some Japanese who had been baptised Christians faced a conflict of loyalty between the Japanese authorities and the church. It may be for these reasons, as well as the need to conquer new territory, that in 1592, Toyotomi Hideyoshi decided to give the unemployed warriors some fighting to do, but not on Japanese soil. His plan was to conquer China and the way into that vast country was to be through Korea. The first of these ventures, in 1592/3 involved around 140,000 men and the second, in 1597/8, about 150,000 men. Although the invasions had considerable military successes, they could not be sustained because the Korean navy disrupted the Japanese supply lines. During the second invasion Toyotomi Hideyoshi sent one of his administrators, Ishida Mitsunari (1560? – 1600) to inspect the forces in Korea. His report criticised Kuroda Yoshitaka (1546 – 1604) and Kobayakawa Hideaki (1577 – 1602) for laxity; it was a report he would later bitterly regret.

While some Japanese ships were ferrying men, food and the matériel of war to Korea, others were venturing into South East Asia to trade. Vessels called *goshuin*, or 'red seal ships' after their official licence, sailed to Annam, Tonkin, Cambodia, Thailand, Taiwan, Malaya and the Philippines trading Japanese produce, particularly swords and staff weapons, for goods such as deer skins, rayskins, feathers, ivory and incense woods. Thousands of masterless *samurai* (*ronin*) with no prospect of fighting in Japan, left their homeland and found employment as bodyguards with the potentates of these countries, and with the European trading factories in them. The king of Thailand in particular had a considerable Japanese bodyguard and at a later date he even appointed a Japanese man, Yamada Nagamasa, as his viceroy.

In 1598, during the second of the Korean invasions, Toyotomi Hideyoshi died, leaving his young son Toyotomi Hideyori (1593 – 1615) in the care of five warrior guardians: Maeda Toshiie, Uesugi Kagekatsu, Mori Terumoto, Ukita Hideie and Tokugawa Ieyasu. He also appointed Ishida Mitsunari, who had sent such a critical report from Korea, as one of five administrators of civil affairs. In 1599 Maeda Toshiie died and Tokugawa Ieyasu moved into Osaka Castle to be close to his young ward, being the most effective intermediary between the child and his other guardians.

The arrival of the first Englishman

On the other side of the world the visit by the four Japanese youths to Europe back in 1582 had not been forgotten. English merchants had considered attempts to trade with Japan from time to time and had persisted in trying to reach Asia by a northern route but had been frustrated by their way being blocked by ice. These ventures were formalised in 1600 by the establishment of the East India Company to finance expeditions to trade in Asia. Another great maritime nation, the Dutch, was also showing considerable interest in the East. The first Dutchmen to reach Japan were part of a fleet of five ships that had set sail to trade in South America. Having rounded Cape Horn they were caught in a violent storm that separated the fleet and blew the ship *Liefde* far from the American coast. After months of hardship crossing the Pacific, the pathetic survivors finally made landfall in the province of Bungo in Kyushu, in April 1600. *Liefde*'s pilot was an Englishman named William Adams, who had taken part in repulsing the Spanish Armada during the reign of Queen Elizabeth. Tokugawa Ieyasu interviewed Adams and was impressed by this Englishman whom he saw as a useful source of knowledge about Europe and a counter to the Portuguese catholics. Adams was eventually made a Tokugawa retainer and although he became very much involved with visiting Europeans, and even made diplomatic voyages for Tokugawa Ieyasu, he was never allowed to return to England.

Japan polarizes

By 1600 the situation inside Osaka Castle was becoming dangerous for Tokugawa Ieyasu. Antagonism against him culminated in an assassination attempt initiated by Ishida Mitsunari. Tokugawa Ieyasu managed to escape the castle and made his way back to his own residence in Edo. Realising he had made a powerful enemy, Ishida Mitsunari began to recruit support, using the safety of the young Toyotomi Hideyori as his excuse. The coalition of *daimyo* and their armies he managed to form became known as the Western Army. In Edo Tokugawa Ieyasu, learning of Ishida Mitsunari's actions rallied his own supporters to form what was to become known as the Eastern Army. Japan was dividing and war between these two great forces became inevitable.

It was Ishida Mitsunari who made the first move, but it was poorly planned. Uesugi Kagekatsu, one of the Toyotomi guardians who had sided with Ishida Mitsunari, held a vast swathe of land to the north of Tokugawa Ieyasu's domain in the Kanto. Ishida Mitsunari felt confident that he would be able to keep Tokugawa Ieyasu occupied on his northern border while the Western Army moved into and consolidated central Japan. At Ishida Mitsunari's request, Uesugi Kagekatsu began a spate of fort building to provoke

Above right: Troops at the battle of Seki ga Hara.

Tokugawa Ieyasu into action. Tokugawa Ieyasu's reaction was to leave the two northern *daimyo*, Date Masamune (1566 – 1636) and Mogami Yoshiaki (1546 – 1614) to deal with the Uesugi while he concentrated on watching Ishida Mitsunari. Ieyasu had already requested that Torii Mototada (1539 – 1600), commanding the garrison of Fushimi Castle, block any attempt by Ishida Mitsunari to move north. Heavily outnumbered, the Torii forces fought off attack after attack before the castle was taken and Torii Mototada committed suicide. They had managed to delay Ishida Mitsunari by ten days and to reduce his army by 3,000. Nobody could have done more. Ishida Mitsunari now had to wait in Ogaki, near Gifu Castle in the province of Mino, whilst other contingents of the Western Army joined him.

On 1 September Tokugawa Ieyasu finally moved. He was keen to prevent the two strategic castles at Gifu and Kiyosu falling into Ishida Mitsunari's hands. Kiyosu was already held by Tokugawa Ieyasu's supporters but Gifu was not, so an advanced party of about 16,000 men was dispatched to reinforce Kiyosu and take Gifu. By the time Tokugawa Ieyasu himself arrived, both castles were securely in the Eastern Army's hands. Unsure how to proceed, Ishida Mitsunari remained at Ogaki, some 16 miles from Gifu to assess the situation. The two castles now under Tokugawa Ieyasu's control dominated the major roads, the Tokaido and the Nakasendo, that were only some 20 miles apart at this point. With Tokugawa Ieyasu in control of this strategic position he could easily overwhelm Ishida Mitsunari. Against all the advice of his military advisors, Ishida Mitsunari decided to move his army so as to block the road south to Osaka and provoke Tokugawa Ieyasu into action. The place he chose for the ambush was a small mountain-ringed cluster of houses at an important junction of the Nakasendo and Hokkokukaido roads some 12 miles from Ogaki, a village called Seki ga Hara.

Above: Detail showing troops at the battle of Seki ga Hara.

Above right: Ishida Mitsunari at Seki ga Hara.

BATTLE OF SEKI GA HARA

Ishida Mitsunari marched his troops out of Ogaki into the teeth of a violent storm, arriving in Seki ga Hara around 1 a.m. on 15 September 1600. Throughout that dreadful night the higher ranks were able to take shelter in the villagers' houses but the troops had to make do with whatever shelter they could find. During the early hours, other contingents of the Western Army arrived and stationed themselves on the hills and valleys surrounding the village. Dawn broke on a scene of utter desolation. Although the rain had finally stopped, the valley was filled with mist and the troops were desperately trying to cook food and dry their clothes and weapons. Tokugawa Ieyasu had delayed moving his troops until about 3 a.m. when the storm had abated, but they were in only slightly better condition than those of the Western Army. By 7.00 a.m. the Eastern Army was still struggling to draw up its battle lines, hampered by the mud and bad visibility. One detachment actually collided with a contingent from the Western Army in the fog but managed to pull away before any real fighting could take place.

Theoretically, Ishida Mitsunari had every advantage, having blocked the roads out of the valley and surrounded the Eastern forces by troops stationed in the surrounding hills and mountains. What he failed to appreciate was that many of his supporters had serious doubts about his intentions and his ability as a military leader. In particular Kobayakawa Hideaki, who still harboured a grudge against him for that critical report from Korea, was in a strong strategic position in the hills to the south. He had indicated to Tokugawa Ieyasu that he might be willing to change sides. Mori Terumoto, who had also been insulted by Ishida Mitsunari, was also less than enthusiastic about fighting for him. Mori Terumoto drew the line at betrayal, deciding instead to hold his position and take as little part in the action as he could.

Finally, at 8.00 a.m. the Eastern Army made its move and the troops opened fire. At the same time Ii Naomasa and about 30 of his men, wearing their distinctive red-lacquered armours, rushed a group of Western Army skirmishers before being joined by the rest of his men in an attack on Ukita Hideie's forces. By noon the Eastern forces although holding their own were becoming anxious that Kobayakawa Hideaki should begin his move. To goad him Tokugawa Ieyasu ordered his troops to open fire on the Kobayakawa forces up on the hillside. Stung into action, 16,000 men swept down the mountain and charged the forces of Otani Yoshitsugu. Other doubters, including the Wakisaka, Kuchiki, Ogawa and Akaza, seeing what was happening also switched sides. The Otani were now hopelessly outnumbered and Otani Yoshitsugu chose to commit suicide rather than face defeat.

Within a relatively short time, the Western Army's fortunes had swung from almost certain victory to certain defeat. Ishida Mitsunari himself decided to break off the engagement and left the field. By 2.00 p.m. only the Shimazu contingent of the once mighty Western Army remained, reduced to 200 men but still fighting. Deciding that further resistance was futile, yet determined not to surrender, Shimazu Yoshihiro ordered his men to attack the Tokugawa forces head on and fight their way straight through them. This tactic was assisted by a suicidal feint led by Shimazu Toyohisa wearing Shimazu Yoshihiro's clothes. Mori Terumoto, whose 30,000 men had stood their ground, but had taken no real part in the battle, slipped away towards Kyushu. By 3.00 p.m. the battle was over and Tokugawa Ieyasu was in total control of the field. Seated on his campstool and surveying the carnage, he made his famous statement: *'It is after the battle that you should tighten the cords of your helmet'.*

Seki ga Hara, 0600, 21 October 1600.
(See page 21 for list of commanders).

The aftermath of Seki ga Hara was terrible. The total number of casualties on the day was 36,000 dead and seriously wounded. Those defeated *daimyo* who had escaped from the battlefield were hunted down and killed, their retainers becoming *ronin*. Ishida Mitsunari himself was captured a few days after the battle and taken to Kyoto where he was beheaded on the Rokujo ga Hara execution ground. In all, the lineages of 87 lords were terminated and their lands confiscated. The villagers of Seki ga Hara, some 900 people, also suffered; their fields were torn up, their houses were destroyed and their harvest for that year totally lost. The dead left lying around the battlefield became a serious health hazard, which the villagers were left to overcome. It took them six months to clear up the debris and bring some semblance of normality back into their lives. For years afterwards travellers would avoid entering the village at night, fearing that the souls of the dead were still abroad.

Tokugawa Ieyasu was now, in effect, the ruler of Japan, but there was still opposition to him. Some *daimyo* he stripped of all title to land, others he reduced their holdings and some were uprooted and moved to territories overlooked by those of his followers. *Daimyo* were divided into three groups: the *shimpan daimyo*, of direct Tokugawa descent, those who had been allies were known as *fudai daimyo* ('inside lords') and those whose loyalty could not be counted on became known as *tozama daimyo* ('outside lords'). For the first time it was established that the term *daimyo* should only be restricted to those nobles whose lands gave them an income of 10,000 *koku* or more per year.

Commander list of Tokugawa Ieyasu (Eastern Army)						
Map ref	Commander	Age	Home Province	Residence	Income (in *Koku**)	No. of Troops
	Horio Tadauji	57	Enshu	Hamamatsu	170,000	5,000
	Nakamura Kazuhide		Fuchu	Numazu	145,000	4,350
	Mizuno Katsushige	36	Mikawa	Kariya	30,000	900
	Nishio Mitsunori	56	Mino	Sone	20,000	600
	Matsushita Shigetsuna	22	Enshu	Hisano	10,000	300
	Hitotsuyanagi Naomori	35	Owari	Kuroda	35,000	1,000
	Tsugaru Tamenobu	51	Mutsu	Hirosaki	45,000	1,000
1	Ikeda Terumasa	37	Mikawa	Yoshida	152,000	4,500
2	Asano Yukinaga	24	Kai	Fuchu	217,000	6,500
3	Yamanouchi Kazutoyo	55	Enshu	Kakegawa	68,600	2,000
	Arima Noriyori	68	Settsu	Arima	10,000	300
4	Arima Toyouji	59	Enshu	Yokosuka	30,000	900
	Wakebe Mitsuyoshi	49	Ise	Ueno	10,000	300
	Tokunaga Nagamasa		Mino	Takamatsu	30,000	900
	Ichihashi Nagakatsu	43	Mino	Imao	10,000	300
5	Tokugawa Ieyasu	59	Kanto	Edo	2,557,000	30,000
	Okubo Hikozaemon	41				
	Honda Masazumi	36				
	Yagyu Munenori	29				
	Okudaira Nobumasa	45				
	Sakai Shigetada	51				
	Matsui Shigekatsu					
	Nishio Yoshitsugu	70				
	Sakai Ietsugu	52				
	Itasaka Bokusai					
6	Fukushima Masanori	39	Owari	Kiyosu	200,000	6,000
	Fukushima Masakatsu	16				
	Fukushima Harushige					
	Kani Saizou					
	Sobue Osai					
	Ono Harunaga					
7	Todo Takatora	45	Iyo	Itajima	83,000	2,500
	Todo Niemon					
8	Kyogoku Takatomo	28	Shinsu	Ina	100,000	3,000
	Tsuda Nobushige	39	Yamashiro	Mimaki	13,000	390
9	Terasawa Hirotaka	37	Hizen	Karatsu	80,000	2,400
	Hachisuka Yoshishige	33	Awa	Tokushima	87,000	5,500
10	Ikoma Kazumasa		Sanuki	Takamatsu	61,000	1,800
11	Kuroda Nagamasa	33	Buzen	Nakatsu	180,000	5,400
	Keya Takehisa					
	Goto Matabei	41				
	Takenaka Shigekado	28	Mino	Iwade	5,000	100
12	Kato Yoshiaki	38	Iyo	Naosaki	100,000	3,000
	Hanawa Dan'emon	34				
13	Tanaka Yoshimasa	52	Mikawa	Okazaki	100,000	3,000
	Tokawa Tatsuyasu		Bizen	Tsuneyama		
14	Tsutsui Sadatsugu	39	Iga	Ueno	95,000	2,800
15	Hosokawa Tadaoki	36	Tanba	Miyazu	170,000	5,000
	Hosokawa Okiaki					
	Hosokawa Masaoki	36	Shimotsuke	Motegi		
16	Ii Naomasa	40	Kozuke	Minowa	120,000	3,000
17	Matsudaira Tadayoshi	21	Bushu	Oshi	100,000	3,000
	Seki Kazumasa	31	Mino	Tara	30,000	900
	Inaba Sadamichi	55	Mino	Gujyo Hachiman	40,000	1,200
	Katoh Sadayasu	18	Mino	Kurono	40,000	1,200
18	Furuta Shigekatsu	41	Ise	Matsusaka	35,000	1,000
19	Oda Yuraku	59	Settsu	Mashita	15,000	450
20	Kanamori Nagachika	75	Hida	Takayama	38,000	1,100
21	Honda Tadakatsu	53	Kazusa	Otaki	100,000	500
	Honda Tadatomo					
22	Togawa Michyasu					400

*Income in *koku* of rice. (1 *koku* was enough to feed 1 man for a year)

Commander list of Ishida Mitsunari (Western Army)						
Map ref	Commander	Age	Home Province	Residence	Income (in *Koku**)	No. of Troops
	Fukuhara Nagataka		Bungo	Niage	60,000	1,800
	Takahashi Mototane		Hyuga	Takanabe	50,000	1,500
	Akizuki Tanenaga	33	Hyuga	Takarabe	30,000	900
	Kakimi Kazunao		Bungo	Tomiku	20,000	600
	Sagara Yorifusa	26	Higo	Kuma	18,000	500
	Kumagai Naomori		Bungo	Aki	15,000	400
	Kimura Katsumasa		Mino	Kitagata	10,000	300
	Kimura Toyomune		Mino	Kitagata		
A	Mori Hidemoto	20	Aki		1,200,000	13,000
	Mori Katsunobu		Buzen	Kokura	60,000	1,800
	Mori Katsunaga					
B	Ankokuji Ekei		Geishu	Hiroshima	60,000	1,800
C	Natsuka Masaie		Gohshu	Minakuchi	50,000	1,500
D	Chosokabe Morichika	26	Tosa	Kohchi	240,000	6,500
E	Ishida Mitsunari	41	Gohshu	Sawayama	194,000	5,800
F	Shima Sakon				20,000	
	Gamou Satoie		Aizu	Aikawa	10,000	
	Mai Hyogo					
	Takano Echu no kami					
	Ohyama Hoki no kami					
	Ujiie Sakubei					
	Kinoshita Nobushige		Harima		20,000	
	Oda Nobutaka		Goshu	Kanzaki	2,700	
	Ito Morimasa		Mino	Ogaki	30,000	900
	Kishida Tadauji		Yamato	Kishida	10,000	300
	Hideyori Kika Kiboroshu					1,000
G	Shimazu Yoshihiro	66	Satsuma	Kagoshima	609,000	800
H	Shimazu Toyohisa	30	Hyuga	Sadowara	28,600	800
	Niiro Tadamoto	69	Satsuma	Okuchi		
	Atachojyuin Moriatsu					
	Yamada Arihide					
I	Ukita Hideie	29	Bizen Bichu	Okayama	574,000	18,000
	Akashi Teruzumi					
	Kawajiri Naotsugu		Mino	Naegi	10,000	300
	Honda Masashige				20,000	600
	Nobuhara Tosa					
	Nishiyama Kunai					
	Asai Senkuro					
	Miyamoto Musashi	18				
J	Konishi Yukinaga		Higo	Uto	240,000	6,800
	Naito Jyoan					
	Sennno Kitasamanosuke					
	Kasuya Saneo	28	Harima	Kakogawa	12,000	360
K	Otani Yoshitsugu	38	Echizen	Tsuruga	50,000	1,500
L	Otani Daigaku					
	Yuasa Gosuke					
L	Kinoshita Yoritsugu	19	Wakasa	Takahama	25,000	700
M	Hiratsuka Tamehiro		Mino	Tarui	12,000	350
M	Toda Shigemasa		Echizen	Yasui	20,000	600
	Takigawa Naiki	58	Izu	Nirayama	20,000	600
N	Gamo Bitchu					1,000
	Matsuno Shigemoto					
	Inaba Masanari					
	Hiraoka Yorikatsu	41				
O	Toyotomi retainers					

Turncoats						
P	Kikkawa Hiroie	38	Izumo	Toda	100,000	3,000
Q	Kobayakawa Hideaki	24	Chikuzen	Najima	522,000	13,000
R	Wakisaka Yasuharu	46	Awaji	Sumoto	33,000	1,000
S	Kutsuki Mototsuna	51	Omi	Kutsuki	20,000	600
T	Ogawa Suketada		Iyo	Imabari	70,000	20,000
U	Akaza Naoyasu		Echizen	Imajyo	20,000	600

Above: Tokugawa Ieyasu commanding his troops during the Summer campaign against Osaka Castle.

Above right: Tokugawa Ieyasu travels by bullock-cart to Kyoto for his appointment to shogun.

On 12 February 1603 the Emperor granted Tokugawa Ieyasu the title of shogun. Chiyoda Castle, his stronghold in Edo, now became the seat of the shogunal court and the city around it grew as merchants and craftsmen flocked to it. He reigned as shogun for only two years, taking the characteristic Japanese step of retiring and sharing the running of the country with his son Shogun Tokugawa Hidetada (1579–1632). Tokugawa Ieyasu chose Sumpu as the site of his retirement home, a familiar location where he had spent his childhood with the Imagawa. Although he filled his days hunting and hawking he was still very much the power in the land. In 1611 he marched into Kyoto with a force of 50,000 to attend the retirement of Emperor Go Yozei. Whilst there he ordered the building of extensions to the imperial palace and had the *daimyo* of western Japan sign a declaration of fealty. A similar pledge of loyalty was extracted from the northern *daimyo* the following year.

English merchants reach Japan

In that same year, 1611, an English trading fleet of three ships left for the Far East with instructions that the commander, Captain John Saris, should continue onwards to Japan should he fail to fill all three vessels with spices. It was late in the season when he finally reached the Spice Islands and he managed to fill only two ships. So as instructed, Saris dispatched the two laden ships back to England and sailed onward himself in the ship *Clove,* landing on the island of Hirado in June 1613. As soon as news of his arrival reached Sumpu, Tokugawa Ieyasu dispatched Will Adams to meet Saris and escort him to Sumpu and ultimately to Edo to meet the shogun. It is clear from Saris's diary that he and Adams did not get on well together, yet despite this Adams played his role as the shogun's representative with professionalism, helping Saris choose suitable gifts and explaining the niceties of Japanese diplomatic protocol.

On their arrival in Sumpu, Saris gave Tokugawa Ieyasu gifts of cloth, gold-decorated guns, and silverware and, rather curiously, a wooden bow made by the ship's carpenter whilst at sea. Both Tokugawa Ieyasu and Adams tried to persuade Saris to set up the English trading station in the Kanto region but he could not be convinced and insisted on using the southern island of Kyushu like the other Europeans. In Edo, Saris was given audience with Shogun Tokugawa Hidetada, again presenting gifts of cloth, guns and silver, but noticeably of lower value than the gift to Tokugawa Ieyasu. In return he was granted the right to trade, and was given gifts for King James I of England including two armours made by Iwai Yosaemon, Tokugawa Ieyasu's personal armourer, a long sword and a number of painted screens. Saris, himself, received a short sword. A footnote to this gift is that when it finally reached London, the members of the East India Company felt that the screens were hardly of a quality suitable for the king and substituted others from their store.

Tokugawa Ieyasu makes contact with the monarchs of Europe

In this same year, 1613, a decision was made to send a delegation from Japan to Spain to obtain permission to trade in Mexico as well as trying to persuade the Spanish to move their trading station northwards to the Kanto. The person chosen to undertake this voyage was Hasekura Tsunenaga, a relatively minor vassal of Date Masamune of Sendai. Both Tokugawa Ieyasu and the shogun provided Hasekura Tsunenaga with gifts for important people in Europe. Hasekura Tsunenaga set sail with Father Luis Sotelo on a ship commanded by the Spanish explorer Sebastian Vizcaino, travelling first

to Mexico, before transferring to another ship bound for Havana and then on to Spain. In Madrid Hasekura Tsunenaga was baptized in the presence of King Philip III, presenting him with many gifts that included armours from Tokugawa Ieyasu. There is documentary evidence that Tokugawa Ieyasu also dispatched two armours to the king of France, despite the fact that the French had no contact with the Japanese. This is corroborated by the fact that two Japanese diplomatic armours appear in the inventory of the French Royal Collection and are still preserved in Paris. Further gifts of armour and weapons were given to the Duke of Piedmont and Savoy who provided Hasekura Tsunenaga with a ship to take him to Rome to meet the Pope. There is little doubt that Tokugawa Ieyasu was, by these gifts, trying to establish links with the rulers of Europe and put Japan firmly on the diplomatic map of the world. However, Hasekura Tsunenaga returned to Japan in 1620 to find this liberal view overturned.

The siege of Osaka Castle

By 1614 Tokugawa Ieyasu was beginning to be concerned about the Europeans and by the political intrigues of the Portuguese in particular. He was also worried about the support being shown to Toyotomi Hideyori, Toyotomi Hideyoshi's son, who was now an adult. Once this concern became widely known it only aggravated the situation and thousands of *ronin*, made masterless at Seki ga Hara and other battles, flocked to Osaka to support the Toyotomi cause.

Osaka Castle, the largest in Japan, had been built by Toyotomi Hideyoshi on the site of the Buddhist temple Ishiyama Hongan-ji, defeated by Oda Nobunaga. At this period the outer works were some 13 kilometres in circumference with moats 300 metres wide, more than adequate to accommodate the 113,800 or so defenders who rallied to the Toyotomi cause. Tokugawa Ieyasu assembled an army of over 190,000 men and marched on Osaka. He had also obtained a large number of cannon from the Europeans, which he used to bombard the castle from the Tokugawa lines. After weeks of siege the attackers had inflicted no real damage on the mighty fortress so Tokugawa Ieyasu made offers of peace. The outcome of these discussions with Toyotomi Hideyori and his mother was that the Tokugawa forces would withdraw provided Toyotomi Hideyori remained in Osaka and agreed to make no further rebellious moves against the Tokugawa. It was also agreed that the outer defences of the castle should be removed. Tokugawa Ieyasu retreated back to Edo feeling confident that he had diffused the situation.

The Toyotomi supporters spent the remainder of that winter and early spring re-excavating the moats, an action that prompted Tokugawa Ieyasu to accuse them of breaking the treaty. Once again *ronin* and other rebels assembled on the pretext of giving support to the Toyotomi line. This time the rebels adopted the strategy of attacking the Tokugawa forces before they reached the Osaka, a decision that had some minor successes. Despite the bravery of the rebels in trying to delay him, Tokugawa Ieyasu finally assembled his army on the outskirts of Osaka. Toyotomi Hideyori felt that it would be unwise to attempt to sit out another siege in a much-weakened castle and decided to commit everything on a major battle in the open. Although the defenders fought valiantly, the might of the Tokugawa forces prevailed and Toyotomi Hideyori finally retreated back to the castle, burned the main tower and together with his mother committed suicide.

Tokagawa Ieyasu becomes a deity

Tokugawa Ieyasu now felt that the Tokugawa line was secure and that the civil war was finally over.

Above: Tokugawa Ieyasu lies ill, with his wife and son in attendance.

Above right: Procession moving Tokugawa Ieyasu's body from Kunozan to Nikko Toshogu Shrine.

There was now no-one strong enough to oppose the Tokugawa and the three branch lines that had been established in Owari, Kii and Mito would supply future shoguns should the main family in Edo fail to produce an heir. In January 1616 Tokugawa Ieyasu fell ill. Whilst on his sickbed Emperor Go-Mizuno-o honoured Lord Tokugawa Ieyasu by conferring on him the title of *Dajyodaijin,* roughly equivalent to the post of a European prime minister and giving control of the politics, judiciary and economics of Japan. On 17 April 1616 Tokugawa Ieyasu died quietly in his bed, content in the knowledge that he had done all he could to ensure the continuation of his lineage.

Shrines are built to honour Tokugawa Ieyasu

He was initially buried at Kunozan Shrine in Shizuoka (formally Sumpu) until his final resting place could be completed according to his will. The place he had chosen for his last resting place was Nikko, in order to comply with the belief that a warrior should be buried to the north of his residence and to protect the provinces of the Kanto Plain. Shogun Tokogawa Hidetada duly built a shrine for his father on the hillside adjacent to the river Daiya, to which Tokugawa Ieyasu's remains were transferred. Emperor Go-Mizuno-o declared that Tokugawa Ieyasu should henceforth be *Tosho Daigongen,* or 'Great Incarnation illuminating the East'. Tokugawa Ieyasu was now a god revered throughout the country.

In 1636 Tokugawa Ieyasu's grandson, Shogun Tokugawa Iemitsu (1604 – 51), rebuilt the original complex of buildings, creating a new shrine of magnificent buildings decorated by the finest artists of their day that has survived virtually unchanged to the present day. Nikko Toshogu Shrine is now a World Heritage Site.

Tokugawa Ieyasu's legacy

Shortly after the battle of Seki ga Hara (1600), Tokugawa Ieyasu summoned various *daimyo* to his court and dispatched others to their domains. By the reign of Shogun Tokugawa Iemitsu this system had been formalized into the *sankin kotai,* whereby every *daimyo* had to spend half his time at the shogun's court and half in their own provinces. The duration and frequency of these visits were varied depending upon whether a *daimyo* was *fudai* or *tozama* and the distance of their province from Edo. Some might have to remain at court six months, others a year. Each *daimyo* had to maintain a residence in Edo where their wives and children had to live permanently. It was these processions between Edo and the provinces that became such a major feature of the Tokugawa era. Depending on the income of their fiefs, the *daimyo* had to provide a suitable entourage that might number thousands. Equipping, feeding and accommodating these numbers for a journey that might take months was, as it was designed to be, enormously expensive. In the case of the Maeda, *Daimyo* of Kaga, a *tozama daimyo* with an income of well over 1,000,000 *koku,* years are recorded when over 3,000 people were involved in the procession. On average the number would be closer to 2,000, broken down into 185 immediate retainers, 830 more distant vassals, 686 servants and pages and 286 grooms and handymen. Such a journey would involve about 32 Kaga horses and 188 horses hired from post stations.

Under the Tokugawa shoguns the stratification of society begun by Toyotomi Hideyoshi was codified and strictly enforced. At the top of the system were the warrior class, the *buke,* followed in order by farmers, artists and craftsmen and finally merchants. Never satisfactorily defined were a few minor categories such as priests, doctors, leather workers and similar groups.

Emphasis was placed on mutual responsibility for good behaviour and the payment of taxes. Should a member of a particular local group fail in some way, retribution fell on the group as a whole. Whilst the Tokugawa shoguns governed the large cities, it was left to the *daimyo* to manage their territories according to broad guidelines set down by the government.

During his life Tokugawa Ieyasu had, by and large, been tolerant of the foreigners in Japan, and had actively sought diplomatic contact with the crowned heads of Europe. His son and especially his grandson Shogun Tokugawa Iemitsu were less tolerant being particularly suspicious of the political ambitions of the Portuguese. In 1638 the Portuguese merchants were forced to move their trading activities to an artificial island called Dejima in Nagasaki Bay. By the following year, after the Japanese had ensured that the Dutch could maintain imports of Chinese silk, the Portuguese were expelled from Japan itself and the Dutch were moved to Dejima to replace them. By this time the English, with little to offer the Japanese other than woollen cloth, had given up hope of establishing a profitable trading base in Japan and had closed their factory.

The closing of Japan

Within a few years Japan had been shut off from the rest of the world, a situation called *sakoku*. The building of ocean-going ships was forbidden and nobody was allowed to leave the country. Anyone who was out of the country at the time of the closure was forbidden to return. The sole exception to this policy of total isolation was that the Dutch were permitted to send one trading ship to Dejima each year. Providing the Dutch were prepared to maintain foreign imports and to supply suitable gifts to the shogun, the Japanese were prepared to tolerate their presence.

With Japan in isolation the Tokugawa government succeeded in imposing a stability that Japan had not seen for centuries. The arts, particularly those cultivated by townsmen, flourished; textiles, lacquer-work, decorative metalwork, ceramics, the theatre and woodblock prints all reached levels of sophistication the world had never seen before. During the 250 years of Tokugawa rule Japan developed in its own way, receiving only a trickle of news of the outside world from the Dutch. Occasionally some exotic foreign import, generally in the form of a gift to the shogun, would cause excitement. In 1725 three Arab stallions arrived in Edo at the request of Tokugawa Yoshimune and a demonstration of Western riding skills was organised. These and later imports of horses were bred with the native horse stock. By the 1760s the Dutch were also importing objects such as electro-static devices and air guns that gave the population of Japan a glimpse of the developments in physics and mechanics taking place in Europe.

The end of an era

By the early 19th century the Japanese learned from the Dutch that the Americans were seeking a coaling base for their steam ships crossing the Pacific, a threat that materialized in 1853 when three warships under the command of Commodore Matthew Perry sailed into Edo Bay. Faced with the shipboard guns and marines armed with the latest rifles, the Japanese could do little. The gunmaking industry in Japan had been virtually closed down centuries before in a deliberate move to prevent the *daimyo* from acquiring these weapons. There was no real alternative but to accept America's demands and open ports to foreign ships. In a matter of only a few years the whole system that had been so carefully maintained by the Tokugawa shogunate for 250 years began to collapse. Although there was

Above: Tokugawa Iemitsu prays for his grandfather, Tokugawa Ieyasu, at Nikko.

Above right: Tokugawa Ieyasu's mausoleum at Nikko Toshogu Shrine.

resistance, the shogun finally abdicated in favour of the emperor and the *daimyo* handed over their power to a central government and to a national army. The rule of the Tokugawa was over but to the Japanese the legacy of Tokugawa Ieyasu was not. Followers of Shinto believe he still resides in Nikko Toshogu Shrine and guides Japan and its people in the modern world, exactly as he did in the years after his victory at Seki ga Hara.

Further reading

Blaker, R 1981 *Needle-watcher: the Will Adams story, British Samurai.* London, Tuttle

Boot, W J 1989 *De dood van een shogun. Oosters genootschap in Nederland 16, Leiden.* Brill, Montreal

Boxer, C R 1951 *The Christian century in Japan 1549–1650.* Berkeley, California

Dower, J W 1971 *The elements of Japanese design.* Tokyo, Whetherhill

Hawley, W M 1990 *Japanese crest design.* California, Hawley Publications

Hickman, M L (ed) 1996 *Japan's golden age – Momoyama.* Dallas, Dallas Museum of Art

Hornung, C 1986 *Traditional Japanese crest designs.* Dover Design Library

Museum of Fine Arts 1989 *The Japan of the shoguns.* Montreal

Sadler, A L 1978 *The maker of modern Japan.* London, Prentice-Hall

Totman, C 1983 *Tokugawa Ieyasu, Shogun: a biography.* San Francisco, Heian

Turnbull, S 1998 *The Samurai sourcebook.* London, Arms and Armour Press

Turnbull, S 1996 *Samurai warfare.* London, Arms and Armour Press

Turnbull, S 1987 *Battles of the Samurai.* London, Arms and Armour Press

Watson, W (ed) 1981 *The great Japan exhibition.* London, Royal Academy of Arts

Yoshinobu T, Shinzaburo O, Toyozo S *et al*, 1983 *The Shogun age exhibition.* Nagoya, Tokugawa Art Museum

JAPANESE HERALDRY

As in Europe, the Japanese used a system of heraldry devised to distinguish friend from foe in the heat of battle. Pictures of battles during the 16th and 17th centuries in particular show that commanders emblazoned their individual badges on their armours, flags, camp curtains and other equipment. Japanese heraldry did not however evolve for battlefield use.

During the Heian period (794–1185) it became the custom for members of the imperial court in Kyoto to decorate their palanquins (sedan chairs), bullock-carts, furniture and other possessions with designs based on flowers, birds and seasonal motifs. Gradually these motifs became more stylized and their use became more formal. From these aristocratic beginnings the use of such symbols spread to the Japanese regions and warrior groups adopted their own symbols to be displayed on their flags. During the Nambokucho period (1336–93), the country was split by civil war. Two emperors laid claim to the throne and the loyalty of their supporters was divided. As father fought son and brother fought brother the need arose for individuals to adopt their own, unique identifying symbol.

Some of the new symbols, known as *kamon* or 'family patterns', were simply variations on what had been used previously but others were totally new creations. Nobody now knows how or why most designs were chosen but legends and stories tell how some originated from specific incidents. One such *kamon*, a circle with two bars across it is supposed to have been inspired by a dish of rice eaten before a battle. It became the custom to grant the use of a *kamon* to a supporter in recognition for their military service. This explains why many unrelated families might use the same design. Even more new *kamon* were adopted during the late 15th century when minor members of the military began to flex their muscles and take over or divide up territories that had previously belonged to aristocratic families. By the time of Lord Tokugawa Ieyasu's birth, anyone who aspired to be of noble birth, or who held land by force of arms would use a distinctive *kamon*.

Following the unification of Japan and the establishment of the Tokugawa shogunate at the battles of Seki ga Hara and Osaka Castle, Japanese society was rigidly divided into four classes: the military, farmers, artisans and merchants. Initially only the military were allowed the use of *kamon*, but by the prosperous Genroku period (1688–1704) this restriction was relaxed and other classes began to adopt them. New patterns were devised that were often witty puns on established designs. Whereas a military family might use a stylised butterfly as its *kamon*, a townsman might imitate it by contorting the leaves and tendrils of a vine into the same shape. By the

Above, and right: Details from a screen depicting the battle of Osaka Castle, 1615.

Left: Examples of *kamon*.

end of the Edo period, all classes of society were using *kamon* and even today they are proudly displayed on ceremonial occasions. Originally there were about 300 basic *kamon*. Today experts recognize about 5,000 but there is no official body, equivalent to the European colleges of arms, to regulate their use.

Most *kamon* are enclosed by a circular frame but other shapes are not uncommon. By far the most popular subjects for *kamon* are flowers and leaves but those depicting animals, objects, characters and geometric patterns are common. One significant difference between Japanese and European heraldry is that of colour. In Europe the colour of the shield, and the charges on it, have specified colours. In Japan the colour is immaterial since a *kamon* might be woven onto brocade, drawn in ink on a lantern or executed in gilded copper on armour. What matters is the design alone. Colour was however important in battle, various units of an army used flags with the same design on them but on different coloured backgrounds.

Battlefield heraldry during the civil wars in Japan is complex. All commanders had *uma jirushi* (horse standards) that indicated their position. These were large, often gilded, three-dimensional objects atop a tall pole and could be almost anything from Lord Tokugawa Ieyasu's golden fan, to black fur-covered discs as used by the Matsuura family. Also used, around the camp, were curtains that shielded the occupants from observation. Many of these were of white cloth with the commander's *kamon* stencilled on them at intervals. Units of the armies were identified by tall narrow flags, of distinctive colour and design. These might have the lord's *kamon* as part of the design but not always, what mattered was that they were sufficiently distinctive to be identified in the smoke and confusion of a battle.

Small flags called *hata sashimono* were flown from poles attached to the backplates of soldiers' armours. These allowed commanders to identify and track the movement of their troops during the course of a battle. Battlefield messengers wore distinctive *sashimono* that were generally of three feather-like flags in bright colours. Lord Tokugawa Ieyasu was unusual in that his messengers had simple white flags marked in black with the character for '5'. Some mounted individuals wore capes called *horo,* attached to the back of their armours, that ballooned out as they galloped. The function of these officials, and others, who wore a feather-like flag diagonally over the left shoulder, is still uncertain.

Kamon still play a role in Japanese society today. On important occasions such as weddings and funerals, when traditional dress is worn, the costumes are still decorated with the wearer's *kamon,* as they have been for centuries. A walk around any neighbourhood in Japan will reveal *kamon* on shrines, temples and other buildings. Even after death, a person's ancestry is proclaimed by a *kamon* on their tombstone.

NIKKO TOSHOGU SHRINE

In his Last Instruction, Lord Tokugawa Ieyasu requested his heirs to 'enshrine my dead body at Kunozan for the first year of my death, and build a small shrine at Nikko and enshrine me there as the God; I will be the guardian of Japan'. In 1617, in accordance with his wishes, his son Tokugawa Hidetada founded the Nikko Toshogu Shrine as his mausoleum. Today there is a common saying in Japan – 'call nothing *kekko* (beautiful, magnificent) until you have seen Nikko'.

The site of the shrine, the mountain town of Nikko ('sunshine'), some 70 miles north of Tokyo, was already a religious centre at the time of Tokugawa Ieyasu.

The main shrine buildings of the Nikko Toshogu Shrine were rebuilt by the third shogun, Tokugawa

Iemitsu in 1636, and represent the climax of the *Gongen-zukuri* (avatar construction) style of Japanese shrine architecture. Although Tokugawa Ieyasu wanted 'a small shrine', Tokugawa Iemitsu's shrine is of majestic size and importance. Contemporary accounts of the construction record that 4,541,230 workmen were involved in its construction, and it took nearly 18 months to complete. The finest craftsmen in Japan

Top: Karamon gate

Above: The Shinkyu, the sacred stable, is decorated with sculptures of monkeys, which were regarded as guardians of horses and it was a custom to keep a monkey in the stable.

Below far left: The parade of warriors at the Spring Grand Festival.

Below left: Three portable shrines or mikoshi, conveying the divine Tokugawa Ieyasu, Totoyomi Hideyoshi and Yoritomo Minamotono, are carried in a procession including the three sacred horses at the Grand Spring Festival.

Above and below right: Horse-archers in action.

Overleaf: The Sacred Bridge at Nikko, taken from the scrolls on the founding of Nikko, by Kano Tanyu, about 1640.

were assigned to the construction of the shrine, which included 568,000 *ryo* (383 kg) of gold and 100 *kan* (375 kg) of silver. Today eight of the shrine buildings are designated as national treasures, while a further 34 are important cultural properties.

Festivals

Spring and Autumn Grand Festivals are held at the shrine each year. These include the *Togyosai* or *Hyakumon-ozoroi Sennin Musha Gyoretsu* ('the hundred articles set, thousand warrior parade'), a ritual that is observed twice annually to keep alive the memory of the arrival of Tokugawa Ieyasu's remains from Kunozan to Nikko in 1617.

Yabusame

On the first day of the Spring Grand Festival *Yabusame* (horse archery) is performed.

Yabusame is the ceremonial art of shooting whistling arrows from a galloping horse at a series of stationary targets. The sport probably started during the Heian period, and is closely related to the ancient horse archery games of mainland Asia.

The current practice of *yabusame* is almost exclusively considered a religious rite: as well as being an offering to the gods, the results of the shooting at the three targets are used in some centres as a divination ritual for the year's harvest.

The *baba* or 'horse track' on which *yabusame* is performed, is straight and 240 metres in length. Three square cedar wood targets or *mato* are inserted diagonally on bamboo poles at about head height, 2 metres from the track at its left side. The first is set 35 metres from the start, and the following two targets are set 75 metres apart, leaving 45 metres at the end of the track to slow the horses down. At the right of the track is a judges' stand, and a target keeper and his assistants sit by each target. The first three *ite* or riders wear medieval-style costume based on medieval hunting gear, and are called *yabusame-ite*. The remaining riders, of which there can be 12 to 17, wear Edo period-style costume, and are called *hiragisha*. Officials at the start and end of the track signal with large fans that the track is clear. The first rider reads a solemn vow from a scroll at the start of the track, and then performs a ceremony called *Age-ogi* in which he tosses a ceremonial fan into the air as he starts his horse. When a hit is scored the target keeper raises a stick with a white paper tassel into the air to signify it. If a rider scores a full set of three hits (*kaichu*), he is presented with a long white silk sash by the master of ceremonies from the judges stand. The broken fragments of the cedar targets are considered lucky, and are signed and dated and distributed after the event as souvenirs.

POLITICAL & SOCIAL BACKGROUND

From this ship for the first time emerged an un-nameable creature, somewhat similar in shape to a human being, but looking rather more like a long-nosed goblin...

Anonymous description of the arrival of a Jesuit priest

In 1543, the year after Matsudaira Takechiyo was born, three Portuguese traders landed on the island of Tanegashima, they were the first Europeans to reach Japan. These merchants carried matchlock muskets, which the Japanese copied and subsequently produced in vast numbers. It was the introduction of the gun that was to break the stalemate of the civil wars.

For almost the next 50 years the Portuguese were the only Europeans to have contact with the Japanese.

1

Folding screen (*byobu*)

Late 16th century

Artist: Kano Takanobu (1571 – 1618)
Wood, lacquer, paper, ink and colours

Nikko Toshogu Shrine

Screens depicting foreigners, and in particular Portuguese merchants and priests, became popular in the late 16th century, some 50 years after the Europeans' first arrival in 1543. The Japanese were fascinated by the dress, speech and deportment of the foreigners and there was a brief vogue for all things European. There was even a fashion for wearing armours that incorporated European elements, particularly cuirasses and open helmets. The armour of Tokugawa Ieyasu, worn by him at the battle of Seki ga Hara, and now preserved as a national treasure at Nikko Toshogu Shrine, is of this type. Like the ships of the Dutch and English who arrived later, the Portuguese landed on the southern island of Kyushu. As a result, all foreigners at that time were known by the rather unflattering name of *namban* or 'southern barbarians'.

Takanobu of Kyoto was the second son of Kano Eitoku and the fifth master of the main Kyoto line of the Kano School. He produced paintings and screens for both Oda Nobunaga and Toyotomi Hideyoshi. Eitoku combined the traditional ink painting of the Kano School with the decorative qualities of the Tosa School, using strong colours on a gold ground to produce art of great vibrancy. Takanobu employed the same style to decorate many of the palaces and castles of the period but, like many of the early Kano artists, much of his work was destroyed during the civil wars. He was *edokoro azukari* (Custodian of the Office of Painting), being employed in 1613 to oversee the screen and wall paintings for the imperial palace in Kyoto. As a reward for this task he was awarded the rank of *Hogen*, 'Eye of the Law', a Buddhist title that was originally the second honorary ecclesiastical rank for priests but was later given to Buddhist sculptors and ultimately to painters. He was the father of Kano Tanyu, Naonobu and Yasudai, three of the greatest of all the Kano artists.

2 Hanging scroll (*kakemono*)

Portrait of Lord Tokugawa Ieyasu

Early 17th century

Artist: Kano Ryotaku
Ink and colours on silk
Nikko Toshogu Shrine

This is one of the large series of posthumous portraits of Tokugawa Ieyasu as a Shinto deity, *Tosho Daigongen*, by the artist Kano Ryotaku. Tokugawa Ieyasu sits on a *tatami* mat wearing court dress of black silk and a slung sword (*tachi*). Above him are hangings decorated with his *aoi mon*, and behind him a landscape.

In the 17th century Nikko became the centre of the cult of *Tosho Daigongen*, and through the agency of the Tokugawa government and the Buddhist priest Tenkai, founding abbot of the Rinnoji temple at Nikko, worship of the former shogun spread throughout Japan. Portraits of this type were distributed to shrines all over Japan as objects of worship. Kano Ryotaku was a Kyoto artist of considerable wealth, who was commissioned by the Nikko Toshogu Shrine to decorate the interior of the innermost shrine of the shrine, the *Hoto*.

3 Woodblock print

Hoeido edition 1833

Artist: Ando Hiroshige (1797 – 1858)
Ink and colour on paper
Blackburn Museum

This print is a view of Okazaki in the province of Mikawa, the birthplace of Tokugawa Ieyasu. The print shows a small procession crossing the bridge and entering the town. The roof of the *daimyo's* castle can be seen in the distance.

Ando Hiroshige was one of the most important of the woodblock print designers, and the greatest of the *ukiyo-e* landscape artists. He was born in Edo, the son of an official in charge of the fire department for Edo Castle, and was trained by Utagawa Toyohiro, giving up his hereditary position in the fire department to spend his time painting and designing prints. In 1833 he produced his famous series *Tokaido Gojosan Tsugi*, or *'Fifty-three stations on the Tokaido'*, the most important road in Japan linking Edo and Kyoto. During his lifetime he is known to have produced about 8,000 prints, sketches and drawings.

4 Flag (*hata sashimono*)

Date uncertain

Hemp fabric

Private Collection

During the period of the civil wars it was customary for commanders to equip each of their infantry soldiers with a flag. These were flown from a pole attached to the backplate of the armour and enabled the troops to be identified at a distance on the battlefield. This example is of hemp, dyed in black with the *kamon* used by the Abe family among others. The bamboo pole to which the flag was attached fitted into a wooden socket that in turn slid into a bracket on the backplate of the armour, behind the shoulders, and into a small cup at the waist.

5 Breastplate (*hara ate*)

Probably 18th century

Iron, lacquer and hemp

Private Collection

This piece of armour, designed to cover only the front of the body, was worn with cross-straps across the back. Its construction and quality suggests that it may have been worn by an officer of foot soldiers under some form of surcoat. The russet iron breastplate carries the *kamon* used by the Nakano family, amongst others, in gold lacquer.

6 Folding armour (*tatami gusoku*)

Probably 18th century

Hemp fabric, lacquer and iron

Royal Armouries XXVIA.288 and Private Collection

Armour made of mail and plates sewn onto a fabric backing was first produced during the civil wars of the early 16th century when large amounts of inexpensive armour was needed for the *ashigaru* or common troops. It was generically known as *tatami gusoku* (folding armour), since it could be stored flat in a relatively small space. This particular example is known as a *karuta gane tatami gusoku,* 'card plate folding armour', since the rectangular plates resemble playing cards introduced to Japan by the Portuguese. Other armours might have hexagonal or other shaped plates. In wear a simple pair of armoured sleeves would have been added. Folding armour continued in production throughout the Edo period.

7 Folding helmet (*chochin kabuto*)

Probably 18th century

Lacquered iron, silk and hemp

Private Collection

The bowl of this helmet is made from a series of interlocking lacquered iron rings connected by silk lacing and kept open by fastening the top plate to a pivoted hoop. When the turn-button is undone the helmet collapses into itself. This ingenious method of construction was one of several devised to reduce the space occupied by munition armour while in storage.

8 Woodblock printed books

Entitled *Zobyo Monogatari*
('Stories of common soldiers')

This edition dated 1846

Artist: Haruta Nobuyoshi
Printing on paper

Private Collection

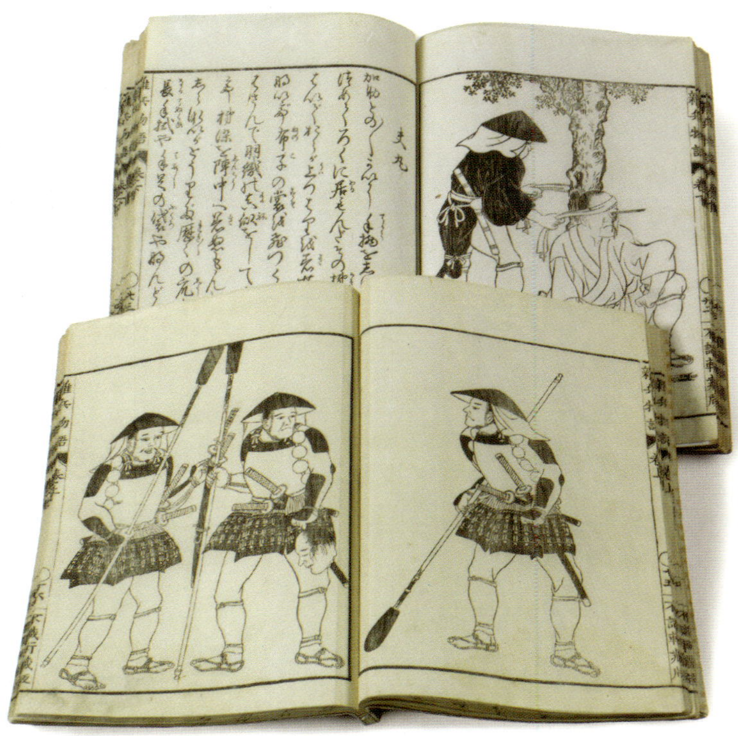

This book, in two volumes, was originally published in the early 17th century as an account of the experiences of common soldiers in the then recent civil wars. It was subsequently reissued many times. Volume 1 is open to show an illustration of spearmen wearing their issued armour consisting of a conical hat of lacquered iron or rawhide, a cuirass of lacquered iron, and armoured sleeves. In reality most of these simple armours would have their lord's device lacquered on the front. Each soldier, depending on his function, would be equipped with a sword and a main weapon, which might be a bow, a spear or a gun. The spherical objects fastened around their shoulders are meals of rice tied into a cloth. One of the soldiers illustrated has a pair of looted swords tied to his spear and is carrying a trophy head for which he will later receive a reward.

Volume 2 is open to show a scene of battlefield surgery to remove an arrow from the eye.

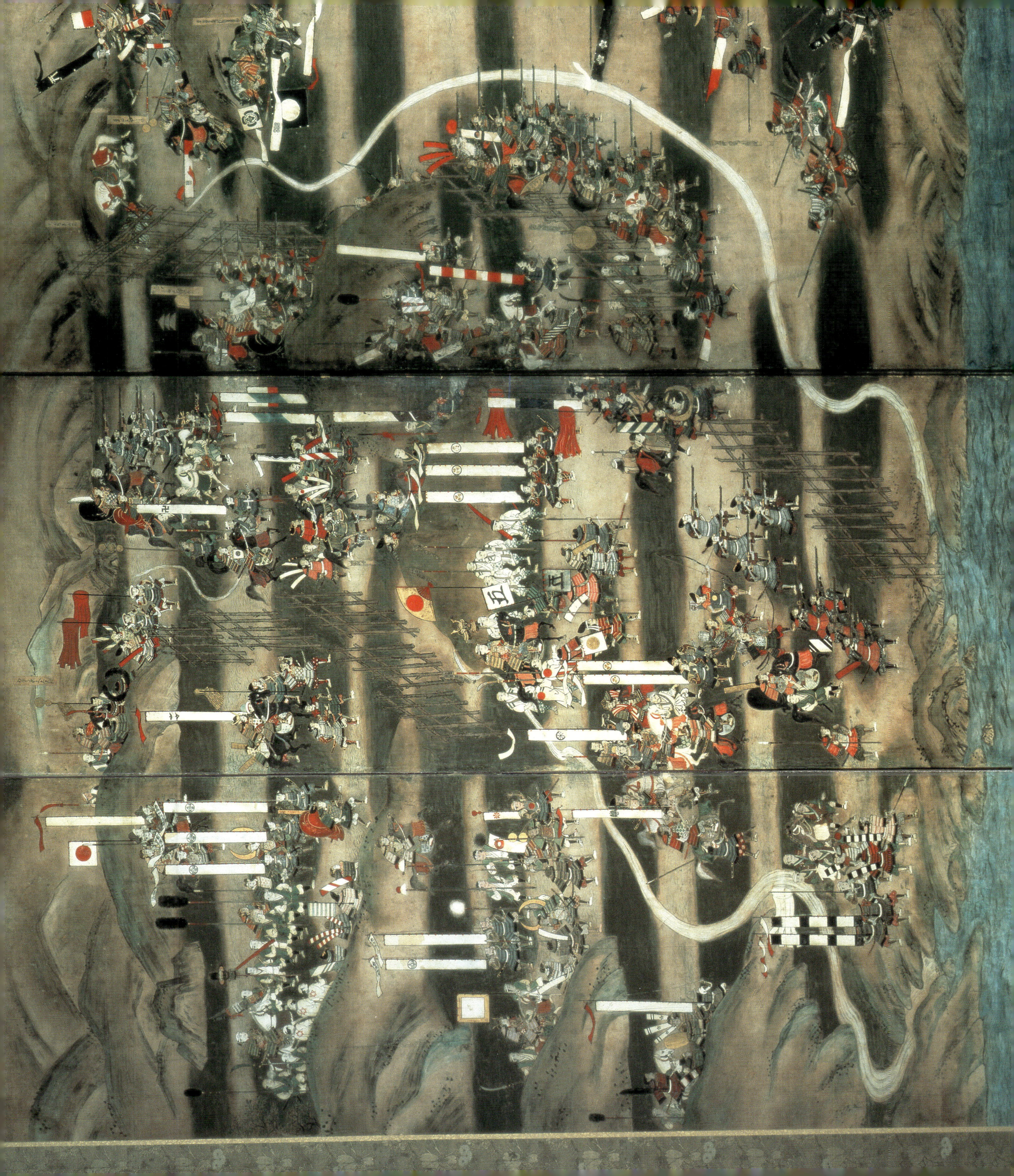

TOKUGAWA IEYASU'S RISE TO POWER

A person's life is like going a long distance with a heavy burden on his back

Tokugawa Ieyasu

On coming of age in 1555 Matsudaira Takechiyo was given the adult name Matsudaira Nobumoto, which he later changed to Matsudaira Motoyasu.

With his father now dead, Matsudaira Motoyasu was the head of the Matsudaira and was expected to fight alongside the forces of their allies, the Imagawa.

In 1560 Oda Nobunaga, a *daimyo* from the province of Owari, attacked the Imagawa army and killed their leader Imagawa Yoshimoto.

Matsudaira Motoyasu formed a new alliance with Oda Nobunaga. He also changed his name again, choosing Tokugawa Ieyasu, the name by which he is known to history.

9 Folding screen (*byobu*)

The battle of Nagashino, 28 June 1575

Early Edo period

Wood, lacquer, paper, ink and colours

Osaka Castle Museum

This screen is a pair to that showing the battle of Nagakute (page 45–47).

The battle of Nagashino actually took place on the field of Shitara ga Hara about a mile from the Tokugawa frontier castle of Nagashino. The castle was under siege by Takeda Katsuyori (1546–82), Lord of Kai province. In response to a messenger who had broken through the Takeda cordon, Oda Nobunaga and Tokugawa Ieyasu raised a coalition army of about 38,000 troops and marched to relieve the garrison. Takeda Katsuyori, against the advice of his senior commanders, insisted on facing this coalition on an open field to take advantage of his cavalry. The Takeda headquarters is shown at the upper right of the screen, marked with a white banner inscribed with the character *dai* or 'great'. The position of the Tokugawa headquarters is to the left of the centre, marked by his golden fan standard.

The actual encounter took place on a late June morning. The alliance had constructed a palisade some distance away from a small stream that divided the battlefield, in the hope that it would lessen the impact of the inevitable Takeda cavalry charge. In front of this barrier were stationed gunners and other troops as 'bait', the remainder being behind it, trained to fire in volleys. In all about 3,000 of the coalition force were armed with guns. As expected, the stream did slow down the horses, around 50 metres or so away from the muzzles of the guns and at the optimum range for a matchlock musket. By rotating the ranks, the musketeers kept up a withering fire that devastated wave after wave of the Takeda forces. In all about 10,000 troops of the once mighty Takeda army were killed and Takeda Katsuyori fled the field.

10 Folding screen (*byobu*)

The battle of Komaki – Nagakute, 15 May 1584

Early Edo period

Wood, lacquer, paper, ink and colours

Osaka Castle Museum

This screen is a pair with that showing the battle of Nagashino (page 42 – 44).

Nagakute was one of a series of battles fought between the forces of Tokugawa Ieyasu and Toyotomi Hideyoshi. Following the assassination of Oda Nobunaga, Toyotomi Hideyoshi (then using the name Hashiba Hideyoshi) had divided the Oda forces by naming Oda Nobunaga's infant grandson as heir and his two surviving sons as guardians. By manipulating the two sons, it became evident that Toyotomi Hideyoshi was planning to take over the whole of the Oda forces and rule through the infant. Toyotomi Hideyoshi dispatched 20,000 men, led by commanders such as Ikeda Nobuteru (1536 – 84), Mori Nagayoshi (1558 – 84) and Oda Nobuo (1558 – 1630), the second son of Oda Nobunaga (1534 – 82), who moved into Mikawa, by-passing the defences. Tokugawa Ieyasu had anticipated this and dispatched his own forces to trail them. After some initial skirmishing, the main armies drew up near the village of Nagakute (now a suburb of Nagoya). Ikeda Nobuteru was killed in the action, as was Mori Nagayoshi who was shot off his horse. Although Toyotomi Hideyoshi himself arrived with reinforcements, neither side was willing to risk the loss of more men and the battle ended without any positive outcome.

五

11 Portrait of Toyotomi Hideyoshi

About 1700

Artist: Fujiwara Kuninobu
Ink and colours on silk

Hideyoshi and Kiyomasa Memorial Museum, City of Nagoya

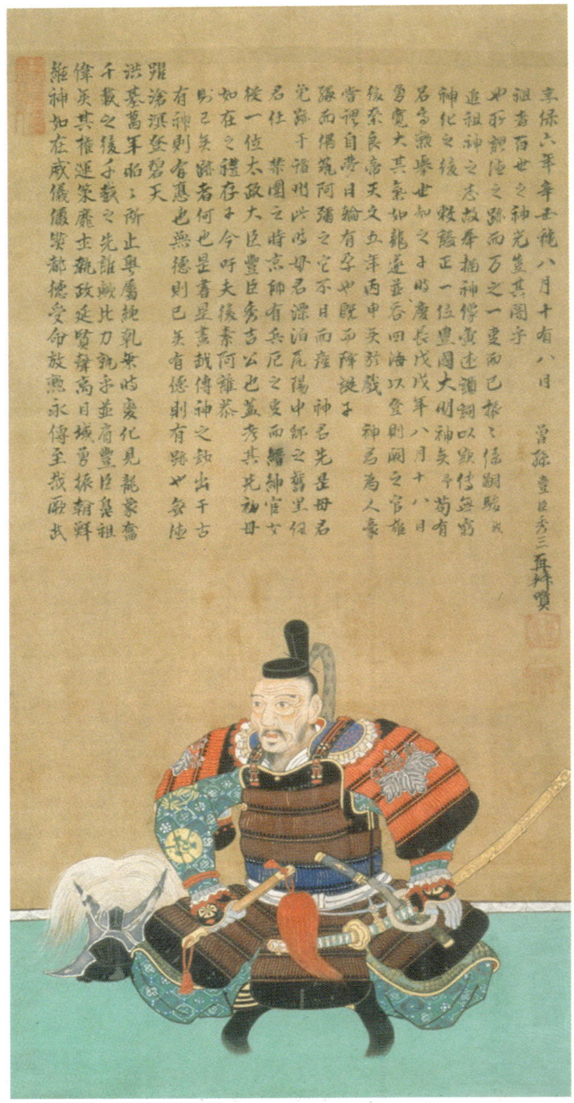

Little is known about the early life of the man known to history as Toyotomi Hideyoshi (1536 – 98). According to tradition he was born in the village of Nakamura in Owari, later serving as a foot soldier for the Imagawa family and subsequently for Oda Nobunaga. By 1564 he was acting as one of Oda Nobunaga's sandal bearers. Six years later he had adopted the surname Hashiba and was commanding a considerable portion of the Oda army. Following the assassination of Oda Nobunaga, Hashiba Hideyoshi avenged his lord and, against some opposition, took control of the Oda forces. Through subjugation and coercion he eventually brought the whole of Japan under his control.

Hashiba Hideyoshi's lowly birth prevented him being appointed shogun, instead the title *Kampaku*, or Imperial Regent, was granted to him in 1585 by Emperor O Gimachi (reigned 1560 – 86). He showered gifts on the imperial court and in return was given the surname Toyotomi or 'Prosperous subject of the Emperor'. His reign was characterized by lavish staged events such as tea ceremonies and cherry blossom viewing parties, to which all of the lords of Japan were invited. In 1592 he received the title *Taiko* or 'Retired Regent' from Emperor Go-Yozei (reigned 1586 – 1611). Some of his social reforms laid the foundation for a strict stratification of society, a prominent feature of Japanese life under the Tokugawas.

In this portrait Toyotomi Hideyoshi is shown as a warrior wearing his brown-laced armour and seated on a mat. He holds a *sai hai*, a tassel of paper attached to a stick that was used by commanders for signalling to their troops in battle. The artist Fujiwara Kuninobu was working around the middle of the Edo period (1603 – 1867).

12 Portrait of Toyotomi Hideyoshi

Replica. Original about 1600

Artist: Unknown
Ink and colours on silk

Osaka Castle Museum

In this portrait Toyotomi Hideyoshi is represented in the formal robes of a Shinto priest as the deity *Hokoku Daimyojin*. Like most of the portraits in this style there is no artist's signature but it follows the conventions established by the Kyoto Kano school of painters whose paintings played a prominent part in the establishment of Toyotomi Hideyoshi as a deity.

This portrait was presented to Kodai-ji temple in Kyoto by Tanaka Yoshimasa, a retainer of Toyotomi Hideyoshi. The colophon was added by the Zen Master Nanke Genko (1538 – 1604), a close friend of Toyotomi Hideyoshi and founder of the Shouji temple in Kyoto, set up to commemorate Toyotomi Hideyoshi after his death.

13 Saddle (*kura*), used by Toyotomi Hideyoshi

Late 16th century

Wood and lacquer

Osaka Castle Museum

Japanese saddles are constructed with a 'tree' of four shaped pieces of wood, usually *kashi,* the Japanese red oak, held together by ties of hemp to give them flexibility. In order to have adequate strength, the front and rear elements are cut from trees that were deformed into a U-shape as saplings; a father prepared the trees that would mature during the lifetime of his son. In use, the saddletree was tied to leather pads to protect the horse and was fitted with a small leather pad for the rider to sit on.

This saddle has a black lacquered ground decorated with gold. Lacquer is the processed sap of a small tree and is obtained, like rubber, by tapping the trunks of mature trees and scraping off the exuded sap. Creating the black ground involves coating the wood with layers of filler and finally multiple coats of lacquer, coloured black with either carbon or iron compounds. The decoration takes the form of the heraldic devices used by Toyotomi Hideyoshi; the Imperial sixteen-petalled chrysanthemum, the *kikumon,* and an arrangement of leaves and flowers of the paulonia tree, the *kirimon.* This form of decoration is known as *maki-e* meaning 'sprinkled picture', and is achieved by dusting the design executed in wet lacquer with powdered gold from a tiny sieve. When the decoration is more or less flush with the surface it is known as *hiramaki-e,* or when raised from the ground by layers of fillers, *takamaki-e.*

14 Lacquered war fan (*gunbai*) of Toyotomi Hideyoshi

Late 16th century

Wood and lacquer

Osaka Castle Museum

Various implements were carried by Japanese commanders for signalling to their troops on the battlefield. One such device, called a *sai hai,* consists of a large tassel of paper or gilded leather attached to a short stick. Other commanders carried fans, either folding or rigid, as here. Many of the folding fans have heavy iron sticks so that they could be used for parrying, or in an emergency as a weapon. The flat fans, called *gunbai,* might be of sheet iron, when they could be used for deflecting arrows or the point of a spear, but were just as often of lacquered wood or rawhide. In a few cases they could be delicate constructions of lacquered gauze stretched on a frame. This example, of gold-lacquered wood, carries the paulonia crest, *kirimon,* granted to Toyotomi Hideyoshi by the emperor.

15 | Cuirass (*do maru*)

About 1500

Iron, rawhide, lacquer, leather and silk

Private Collection

All armour used before the civil wars in Japan was of lamellar construction, that is made up from small, overlapping plates of either rawhide or iron, which were lacquered, and then laced together with silk braid to form a component of an armour. This style of cuirass in which the rows of lamellae open under the right arm is known as a *do maru*, or 'around the body'.

This *do maru* is in an older style, but of a type that continued to be worn during the period of the civil wars. It has the older form of flat upper plates on the chest and under the arms that did not have a turned over edge to deflect the points of weapons. Internally each row of lamellae are individually wrapped in leather as a lining. The *kusazuri,* the pendant sections covering the hips and upper legs, are attached to the lower edge of the *do* proper by short lacing and are divided into eleven sections for ease of movement.

16 | Cuirass (*do maru*), associated with Toyotomi Hideyoshi

Late 16th century

Iron, rawhide, lacquer and silk

Osaka Castle Museum

By the 16th century lamellar armour was being replaced by armour of rawhide or iron plates, often lacquered to look like lamellae. Nevertheless lamellar armour continued to be made, particularly for the nobility. They still however often incorporated details that had become standard for plate armour. This cuirass for example differs from older *do maru* in having five instead of the traditional four rows of lamellae around the trunk, giving greater protection to the lower abdomen and transferring some of the weight onto the hips rather than to the waist. Another change was to the solid iron plates at the top of the scale sections that are shaped to the neck and arm and have an outward turn to deflect the point of a weapon, rather than being flat and angular as previously. These plates on this armour, and the lowest plates on the *kusazuri* covering the hips and upper thighs, are decorated in gold lacquer with the *kamon* used by Toyotomi Hideyoshi; the flowers and leaves of the paulonia tree, the *kirimon,* and the chrysanthemum or *kikumon,* both symbols granted by the emperor.

15 ▸

17 Portrait of Honda Tadakatsu

Early 17th century

Artist: Unknown
Ink and colours on silk
Tachisaka Shrine

Honda Tadakatsu (1548–1610), a close companion of Tokugawa Ieyasu and one of his four loyal retainers, the *Shitenno*, acted as a commander in all of his campaigns. He can be identified on many battle screens wearing the same black armour, with its large black-lacquered deer's antler crests on the helmet, which he wears in this portrait. In 1590 he was made a *daimyo*, being granted the fief of Otaki with an income of 100,000 *koku* of rice (1 *koku* being approximately the amount of rice needed to feed one man for one year). For his assistance at the battle of Seki ga Hara, Tokugawa Ieyasu granted him Kuwana in Ise province, with an income of 150,000 *koku*.

Unlike most Japanese portraits, which emphasized the secular or religious nature of the sitter by depicting them seated on mats wearing court or priestly robes, in this image Honda Tadakatsu is depicted as the very model of a warrior. He is shown in his armour with an exaggerated Buddhist rosary around his cuirass, seated on a campstool, leaning forward in an assertive pose.

18 Set of books outlining the history of the Tokugawa family

Completed in 1843

Authors: Hayashi Jyusai and Narishima Motonao
Printing on paper
Nikko Toshogu Shrine

In 1566 Mastudaira Motoyasu applied to Kyoto for permission to change his family name. He eventually settled on the name Tokugawa Ieyasu, finally ridding him of all association with Imagawa Yoshimoto, with whom he had lived as a child, and for whom he had fought on attaining manhood. As was customary at the time for any person of rank, Tokugawa Ieyasu established his pedigree, tracing it from the Nitta family and through them to the Minamoto clan and to the shoguns of the early medieval period. His new family name, Tokugawa, was derived from a place name associated with his ancestors.

This set of ten books details the origins of the Tokugawa family and its subsequent history. It was commissioned by Tokugawa Ienari (reigned 1787–1837) from Hyashi Jyusai and Narishima Motonao. They took 34 years between 1809 and 1843 to complete the work.

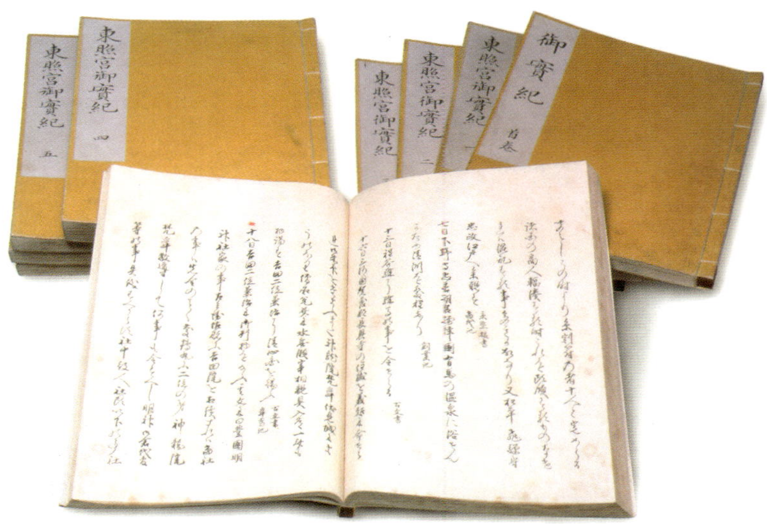

BATTLE OF SEKI GA HARA

the summer grasses
all that remains
of brave soldiers dreams

Basho

The two armies eventually met in October 1600 near the small village of Seki ga Hara in central Japan. Most of the troops arrived at the battlefield during a night of torrential rain and violent winds. By morning the rain had stopped but a heavy mist hung over the village making the identification of the flags and banners difficult. Ishida Mitsunari's Western Army, with about 110,000 troops, blocked the roads out of the valley and had other troops stationed on the wooded slopes of the encircling hills. Tokugawa Ieyasu's Eastern Army, of about 115,000 men, was mainly strung out along the valley floor.

19 Folding screen (*byobu*)

The battle of Seki ga Hara 1600

Replica, about 1854

Copy of an original thought to be by Kano Baishun
Wood, paper, ink and colours

Folklore and History Museum, Seki ga Hara

The battle of Seki ga Hara took place on 15 September 1600 between the forces allied to Tokugawa Ieyasu and those supporting the young son of Toyotomi Hideyoshi led by Ishida Mitsunari. Seki ga Hara itself was a relatively small village at an important point on the Nakasendo road where a branch road joined with the Tokaido road. Ishida Mitsunari had positioned forces of the Western Army across the road leading out of the valley as well as on the hills to either side. Other Western units were stationed in side-valleys, well to the rear, to block off any attempt by Tokugawa Ieyasu and the Eastern Army to escape. Although it seemed that Tokugawa Ieyasu would walk into the trap, he had learned about past differences between some of the Western Army commanders and Ishida Mitsunari and used them to his advantage. In particular Ieyasu learned that Kobayakawa Hideaki, with some 13,000 men positioned on the hillside above the valley, had decided to change sides during the battle. Other disgruntled commanders, whilst not prepared to actually betray Ishida Mitsunari, had decided to take no part in the action.

The screen shows a representation of the battle with the Tokugawa headquarters in the lower right corner and Ishida Mitsunari's position at the upper centre. Prominent, in a band towards the left of the screen, are the forces of Ii Naomasa in their characteristic red-lacquered armours. The Kobayakawa forces, and other turncoats, are only partially shown in the lower left corner.

20 | Helmet (*kabuto*)

Early 17th century

Iron, wood, leather, lacquer and silk

Kunozan Toshogu Shrine

This helmet was worn by the third Tokugawa shogun, Iemitsu (1604–51), the grandson of Tokugawa Ieyasu. It takes the form of a tall, angular, fabric cap, the ties of the hood being represented by a crest attached to the rear of the bowl. During the period of the civil wars and for a short time later, it was common for warriors to wear distinctive armour, and in particular elaborate helmets, so that they stood out on the battlefield and their deeds were noticed. In many cases, a novel helmet shape was achieved by adding a superstructure of paper, lacquer and wood to a simple iron helmet bowl to create what is known as a *harikake kabuto*; all unusual helmets being known as *kawari kabuto*. The mask that belongs to this helmet has survived but is in a very fragile condition and is not displayed.

21 Helmet (*zunari kabuto*) and mask of the Ii family

Late 16th century

Iron, lacquer, silk and leather

Royal Armouries XXVIA.224

During the late 15th century armourers were faced with the problem of having to produce large quantities of armour at a reasonable price for issue to the armies of the *daimyos*. One innovation was to simplify helmet construction. Previously all helmets had been made from a number of plates arranged like the triangular panels of a cap. Although not the inventors, Hineno Hironari and his brother Yajiuemon developed and popularised this style, called *zunari kabuto*, or 'head-shaped helmet'. Being of simple construction, thousands could be turned out in thin plate for common troops and in thicker plate for men of rank. This helmet is fitted with a split neck guard, known as a *gessan jikoro*, a popular style at this period. Unlike a normal neck guard of continuous plates that trapped the blade of a spear and deflected it onto the neck, this construction allowed such a spear to pass harmlessly through the gaps.

The red lacquer and the gold fore-crest, (now badly damaged) indicate that this helmet was made for the Ii family of Hikone. It also has a fitting for some form of crest at the rear, but there is no indication of what that might have been.

22 Helmet (*kabuto*) and mask (*mempo*)

Helmet bowl 16th century

Manufacturer: Haruta School
Iron, leather, wood and silk

Private Collection

It was common in Japan for fine pieces of armour to be recycled. This example has a helmet bowl dating from the late 16th century that has been fitted with a neck guard and crests during the Edo period (1603 – 1867). The bowl, probably made by the Haruta family of armourers, represents a head wearing a type of court cap. The rectangular hole in the peak, and blocked holes on the brow plate, suggest that the bowl was originally fitted with some form of nasal bar, a form of face defence that is otherwise unknown on helmets from Japan. The present crests consist of a fore-crest, *maedate*, of lacquered wood and a pair of side-crests, *wakidate*, that take the form of exaggerated *fukigayeshi*, the characteristic turn-backs of the front edge of the neck guard of a Japanese helmet.

The mask, which has a bushy moustache of yak hair, defended the face but also provided secure anchor points for the helmet cord.

During the attempted Mongol invasions of the 13th century the Japanese were bombarded by ceramic pots filled with gunpowder and fragments of iron launched from catapults. Although literary references are scarce, there is some documentary evidence that similar weapons were used by the Japanese during the Onin War (1467 – 77). In 1510 a Chinese gun was imported into Sakai and a few copies were made, but unfortunately there is no evidence or surviving example to show what it was like. The guns that arrived with the Portuguese in 1543, on the other hand, had a profound effect, and within a decade they were being made in numbers that allowed Oda Nobuhide to acquire 500 guns for his bodyguard. Within twenty years or so towns such as Sakai, Kunitomo and Nagahama were producing thousands of matchlock muskets.

Almost all Japanese guns were snapping matchlocks; in which the charge in the barrel was ignited by a glowing length of match cord impregnated with saltpetre. In addition, the arm that held the match was 'cocked' against a spring, snapping into the priming charge in the pan on pulling the trigger.

23 Large-bore matchlock gun (*hinawa ju*)

Edo period (1603 – 1867)

Signed by Noda Jinbei
Iron, copper alloy and wood
Folklore and History Museum, Seki ga Hara

Large-bore guns such as this example were used to batter down doors or for launching fire grenades. Noda Jinbei, the maker of this gun, is unrecorded, but other members of the Noda group are known to have worked in the province of Settsu, modern Hyogo Prefecture.

24 Large-bore matchlock gun (*hinawa ju*)

Edo period (1603 – 1867)

Iron, copper alloy and wood
Royal Armouries XXVIF.209

This particular gun has lost its lock, trigger and trigger guard. The barrel is decorated with the Tokugawa *kamon* and is inlaid in silver with the characters for 'whirlpool' or 'abyss'.

25 ▸

26 ▸

25 Matchlock gun (*hinawa ju*)

Momoyama/early Edo period

Manufacturer: Kunitomo Tobei of Omi Province
Iron, copper alloy and wood

Nagahama Castle Historical Museum

The Kunitomo group of gun makers made vast quantities of matchlock muskets for the civil wars, many of the guns used in the siege of Osaka Castle being ordered by the Tokugawa from the Kunitomo. Much of their work was characterized by its simplicity of construction and lack of decoration. They were capable of very good work, but some of their munition guns were less satisfactory and gained the nickname '*udon ju*' – they were likened to egg noodles because the barrels bent and flexed when fired. Japanese gun makers standardized the calibres of their guns, long before it was common in Europe, making the provisioning of ammunition simpler. The system they used was to state the weight of a ball of lead that fitted the barrel in *momme* (1 *momme* = 3.75 g). This gun having a bore of 1.2 cm, is described as a '3 *momme* gun'.

26 Matchlock gun (*hinawa ju*)

Momoyama/early Edo period

Manufacturer: Jinroku Takakura
Iron, copper alloy and wood

Nagoya Castle

Because many guns were produced as part of large munitions orders, they were not signed by their makers, making dating and identification difficult. Although this example is signed by the manufacturer it remains typical of the guns used in the civil wars, but could be later.

27 Three portraits of Tokugawa Ieyasu and his two generals

About 1930

Artist: Kobori Tomoto
Ink and colours on paper
Nikko Toshogu Shrine

This set of three portraits depicts Tokugawa Ieyasu in the centre, Honda Tadakatsu (1548 – 1610) on the left and Ii Naotaka (1590 – 1659) on the right. All are shown wearing their armours, seated under their standards, *uma jirushi*.

Tokugawa Ieyasu is shown wearing his famous *namban gusoku,* now preserved at Nikko Toshogu Shrine; an armour he wore at Seki ga Hara that incorporates European elements. The cuirass is probably Flemish about 1585 and is of peascod shape, rough from the hammer and decorated with chiselled lines. It is worn with a gorget (neck guard) that has been extended in Japan so that it could be worn outside the cuirass, as a piece of armour the Japanese called a *manchira,* a corruption of the Spanish for cape. Considerable quantities of these munition armours were produced for the troops in the Spanish Low Countries and these elements were probably imported by the Dutch. Mounted on a pole is the helmet that takes the form of a 'Spanish morion' fitted with a neck guard in the Japanese manner. Behind Tokugawa Ieyasu is his *uma jirushi,* a golden fan (see page 63).

Honda Tadakatsu is shown wearing his characteristic black armour with large antler side crests fitted to the helmet and an exaggerated Buddhist rosary over one shoulder.

Ii Naotaka, the second son of Ii Naomasa (1561 – 1602), took part in the siege of Osaka Castle after his elder brother had refused to fight. Because of this he was granted his brother's domain. He is shown wearing a typical Ii family armour, lacquered red and fitted with tall gold crests similar to that included in the exhibition (see page 58).

This set of pictures was presented to Nikko Toshogu Shrine by the artist in 1930.

28 War standard (*uma jirushi*) of Lord Tokugawa Ieyasu

Late 16th century

Paper, bamboo and gold

Kunozan Toshogu Shrine

Uma jirushi or 'horse standards' were displayed next to commanders during a battle, indicated their position and acted as rallying points. Many take the form of a gilded ornament fastened to the top of a pole with long cloth streamers attached to it. That used by Toyotomi Hideyoshi was topped by a cluster of gilded gourds fastened on wires.

This *uma jirushi*, used by Tokugawa Ieyasu in all of his major battles, and visible on the Nagakute, Nagashino and Seki ga Hara battle-screens, takes the form of a large folding fan made of bamboo and gilded paper. Some later paintings show the fan as having a red sun painted on it, but there is now no evidence for this. The fan was originally carried and displayed on a 5.73 metre tall bamboo pole that is now lost.

29 Sword mounting (*tachi*)

In the style of the 16th century

Wood, lacquer, iron, copper alloy, leather, rayskin and silk

Royal Armouries XXVIS.397

All early long swords were mounted as *tachi* and slung edge downward on the left hip. By the time of Seki ga Hara many found it more convenient to wear their long sword thrust through their sash on the left, although the *tachi* continued to be used by the higher ranks and remained so until the wearing of swords was abandoned.

This mounting is probably a 19th-century copy in the style of the 16th century. The scabbard is of lacquered wood, reinforced by iron fittings and fastened to the body by a partially gilded leather tie. The hilt, also of wood, is covered with rayskin and then wrapped with variegated silk braid. The swordguard, *tsuba*, is of bronze.

30 | Sword blade (*katana*)

About 1590

Manufacturer: Fujiwara Kanemichi
Steel
Nikko Toshogu Shrine

This blade is for a *katana*, worn edge upward through a sash on the left hip. When the sword is being worn the signature should be on the side of the tang facing outwards.

Kanemichi was one of four brothers who were moved from Seki in Mino province to Kyoto by their father, also called Kanemichi, around 1560. Their family name was Mishina. Around 1595 the eldest son, who made this blade, was granted the honorary title *Iga no Kami* (Governor of the province of Iga). Like many blades in the collection of Nikko Toshogu Shrine, it was damaged during the 19th century by a fire that destroyed a storehouse. The blade has been re-hardened by a modern smith and re-polished to recapture some of its former glory.

31 | Blade (*naginata*)

About 1300

Manufacturer: Bishu Osafune Kagemitsu
Steel
Nikko Toshogu Shrine

Naginata were staff weapons fitted with curved single-edged blades similar to the European glaive. Very early *naginata* generally had long blades and proportionally shorter shafts than those made later. By the Edo period even lighter *naginata* were made for use by the women of military households. *Naginata* (which means 'mowing down sword') were used in swinging circular cuts capable of devastating effect.

Kagemitsu was a smith working in the village of Osafune in the province of Bizen, a centre populated almost entirely by swordsmiths. He worked around the beginning of the 14th century and many of his surviving works are regarded as national treasures in Japan. This blade was another of those damaged in the 19th century storehouse fire and has had to be re-hardened by a modern smith.

32 | Sword blade (*katana*)

About 1210

Manufacturer: Bitchu Tsuguie
Steel
Nikko Toshogu Shrine

The smith who forged this blade lived in the province of Bitchu and was the grandson of the founder of a group of swordsmiths who used the name Aoe or Aoii, a group that established a reputation for quality. Tsuguie was one of a number of smiths who attended the retired Emperor Go Toba (reigned 1185 – 98) and taught him sword making. It is probable that Go Toba did not actually forge the blades himself but attended the forging and then carried out the hardening under the sword maker's direction.

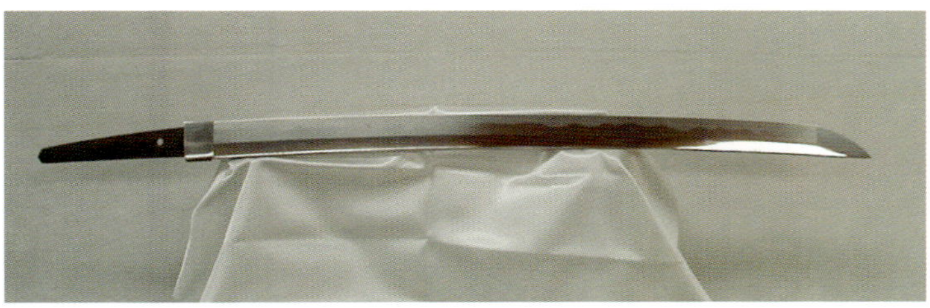

30 ▸

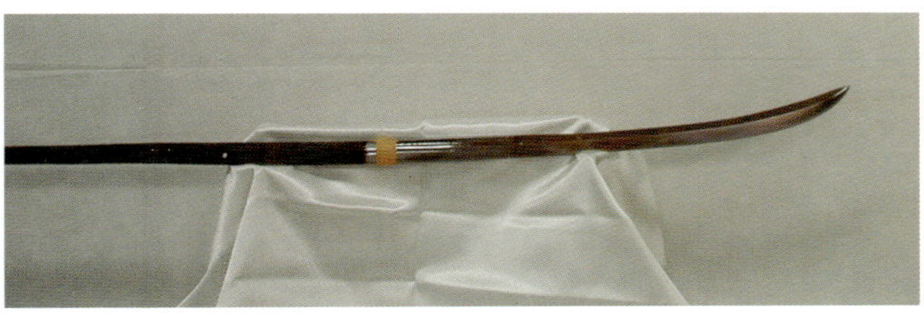

31 ▸

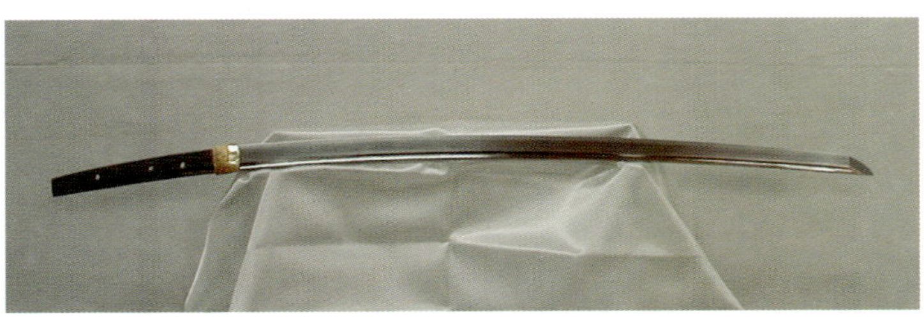

32 ▸

33 Armour (*tosei gusoku*) of the Sakakibara family

About 1600

Iron, rawhide, lacquer, leather, silk and bear fur

Royal Armouries XXVIA. 274

Sakakibara Yasumasa (1548 – 1606) was one of Tokugawa Ieyasu's *Shitenno*, or trusted commanders. The character 'Yasu' in his name being granted by Tokugawa Ieyasu. After Seki ga Hara, Sakakibara Yasumasa, realizing that there would be little or no fighting in the immediate future, retired. Several of Yasumasa's armours survive in Japan, one of which incorporates European elements. This armour is of approximately the same period and has essentially the same *kamon* (the wheel of a bullock cart) as used by Sakakibara Yasumasa, the difference being the addition of an axle and wedge in the centre of the wheel. Yasumasa had a son called Sakakibara Yasukatsu and an adopted son Yorinao, both of whom fought at the siege of Osaka Castle as supporters of the Tokugawa. It is likely that this armour belonged to one of them.

The helmet is in a style known as an *akodanari kabuto*, named after its supposed similarity in shape to the upper part of a pumpkin, and was rather old fashioned by the time the armour was made. The cuirass and other elements are of solid iron plates that are lacquered and laced to resemble lamellae, a construction known as *kiritsuke kozane*, (cut-out and stuck-on scales). The bear bristles that adorn the lower edge of the main elements assisted in shedding rain.

34 Armour (*tosei gusoku*) of the Ii family

About 1800

Iron, lacquer, leather and silk

Hikone Castle Museum

It was traditional in the Ii family for successive generations to have their armours modelled on that worn by Ii Naomasa (1561 – 1602), the 24th head of the family and one of Tokugawa Ieyasu's *Shitenno*, or senior commanders, who was given a fief in Omi province after the battle of Seki ga Hara.

Ii Naomasa had admired a red-lacquered armour being worn by Yamagata Masakage (d.1575) and decided to have his armours decorated in the same way. All subsequent Ii armours, both for the *daimyo* himself, and those of his troops, were similarly red lacquered. The family also adopted a tall pair of 'horns' in gold as the crest for their helmets. This armour was made for Ii Naonaka (1789 – 1812), differing from Ii Naomasa's original armour only in that it is laced in a different colour, Ii Naomasa's being laced in dark blue. The armour features a *zunari kabuto*, a 'head-shaped helmet' with eyebrows embossed on the peak, and a cuirass that the Japanese describe as a *dangaye do*, that is one with areas laced in different styles.

35 Saddle (*kura*) and stirrups (*abumi*)

Dated 1662

Manufacturer: Masaya
Wood, iron and lacquer

Hikone Castle Museum

This set of saddle and matching stirrups is decorated with the *aoi mon* of the Tokugawa family, as well as chrysanthemums and foliage in gold and silver lacquer on a black lacquered ground. The characteristic open-sided Japanese stirrup developed during the early Heian period (794–898) from a type of boot-stirrup that enclosed the whole front of the foot. By omitting the side pieces and extending the base plate, a stirrup was created that suited the principal method of fighting in Japan at the time, shooting with a bow from horseback. Even though mounted archery declined in actual warfare, it continued to be practiced at shrines, as *yabusame*, to entertain the Gods. This style of stirrup continued to be used until the introduction of European forms in the 19th century. Some stirrups are made from lacquered wood, reinforced by iron strips whilst others are of solid iron and of considerable weight.

This saddle is inscribed with the name Masaya who worked for the shogun's court during the 17th century.

36 | Saddle (*kura*) and stirrups (*abumi*)

Dated 1682

Manufacturer: Sadafusa
Wood, iron and lacquer
Hikone Castle Museum

This saddle is simply decorated with the *aoi mon* of the Tokugawa family in gold and silver lacquer on a polished black lacquered ground. It is inscribed to the effect that it was made by Sadafusa, the 10th master of the Ise school of saddlers. Unusually the stirrups are of plain black lacquer, relieved only by the piercing of a leaf from the arrowhead plant (*omodaka*) outlined in gold lacquer.

37 Picture scroll

Lord Tokugawa Ieyasu and his twenty loyal retainers

Edo period (1603 – 1867)

Ink and colour on silk

Nikko Toshogu Shrine

In this scroll painting, Tokugawa Ieyasu is depicted, seated on a camp stool, with twenty of his senior retainers. These are:

1. Matsudaira Ietada
2. Honda Tadakatsu
3. Hiraiwa Chikayoshi
4. Sakakibara Yasumasa
5. Shimaya Mitsutada
6. Okubo Tadao
7. Watanabe Moritsuna
8. Naito Masanari
9. Hatori Masanari
10. Mizuno Tadashige
11. Ando Naotsugu
12. Sakai Tadatsugu
13. Yonezu Katsumasa
14. Ii Naomasa
15. Osuka Yasutaka
16. Takaki Masatsugu
17. Okubo Tadasuke
18. Toda Tadatsugu
19. Karuoku Chikakane
20. Atsumi Katsuyoshi

38 Picture scroll

Lord Tokugawa Ieyasu and his sixteen retainers

Edo period (1603 – 1867)

Artist: Kanemura
Ink and colour on paper

Association for the Advancement of Nagoya Castle

This painting is one of several that illustrate Tokugawa Ieyasu (seated at the top) with his major commanders. It should be compared with that from Nikko Toshogu Shrine that depicts twenty retainers.

39 Pair of riding gloves (*tebukoro*)

Early 17th century

Leather

Kunozan Toshogu Shrine

When riding, or when wearing armour, it was usual to wear a pair of soft leather gloves. These examples were the property of Tokugawa Iemitsu, Tokugawa Ieyasu's grandson, and have the Tokugawa crest on the backs. It was usual on such gloves for the two central fingers to be made from a different leather.

40 Shoulder guards (*o-sode*)

About 1500

Iron, rawhide, lacquer, silk, gilded copper alloy and silver

Royal Armouries XXVIA.329

Lamellar armour, made from small plates of rawhide and iron laced together with leather and silk, had been largely replaced by the middle of the 16th century by armours of plate. Similarly, most had given up wearing these large shoulder guards although they continued to be worn by people of rank because of their imposing appearance. Shoulder guards were originally designed to act as 'shields' when mounted archery was the normal form of warfare, leaving both hands free to use the bow. The complex system of cords and ties with which they were attached to the cuirass held them securely in position yet allowed complete freedom of movement to the arms.

This pair of *sode* must have belonged to a particularly rich armour. The silver *kamon* decorating the black-lacquered top plate was used by the Watanabe family, amongst others.

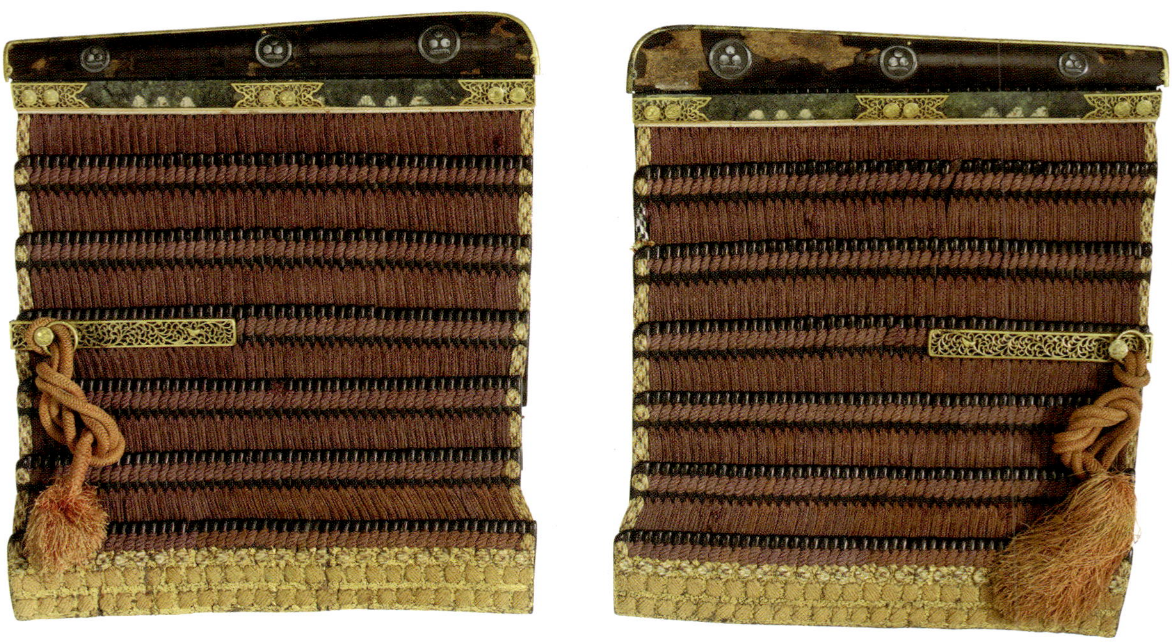

41 Picture scroll of the battle of Seki ga Hara (*e-maki*)

Dated 1831

Ink and colour on paper

Association for the Advancement of Nagoya Castle

This scroll depicts the series of preliminary actions leading up to the battle of Seki ga Hara. Prior to the battle itself, Ishida Mitsunari had induced one of his supporters, Uesugi Kagekatsu, to provoke Tokugawa Ieyasu by building a series of forts on his northern border, while Ishida Mitsunari himself moved his army into central Japan, hoping to take control of various important roads in that area. Instead of acting as Ishida Mitsunari expected, Tokugawa Ieyasu left Uesugi Kagekatsu to be dealt with by two of his allies and marched into central Japan himself.

By capturing strategically important castles that dominated the main Tokaido and Nakasendo roads Tokugawa Ieyasu established his hold on the area, forcing Ishida Mitsunari to take a stand at Seki ga Hara.

The forces depicted in the centre of the scene illustrated here are those of Ishida Mitsunari.

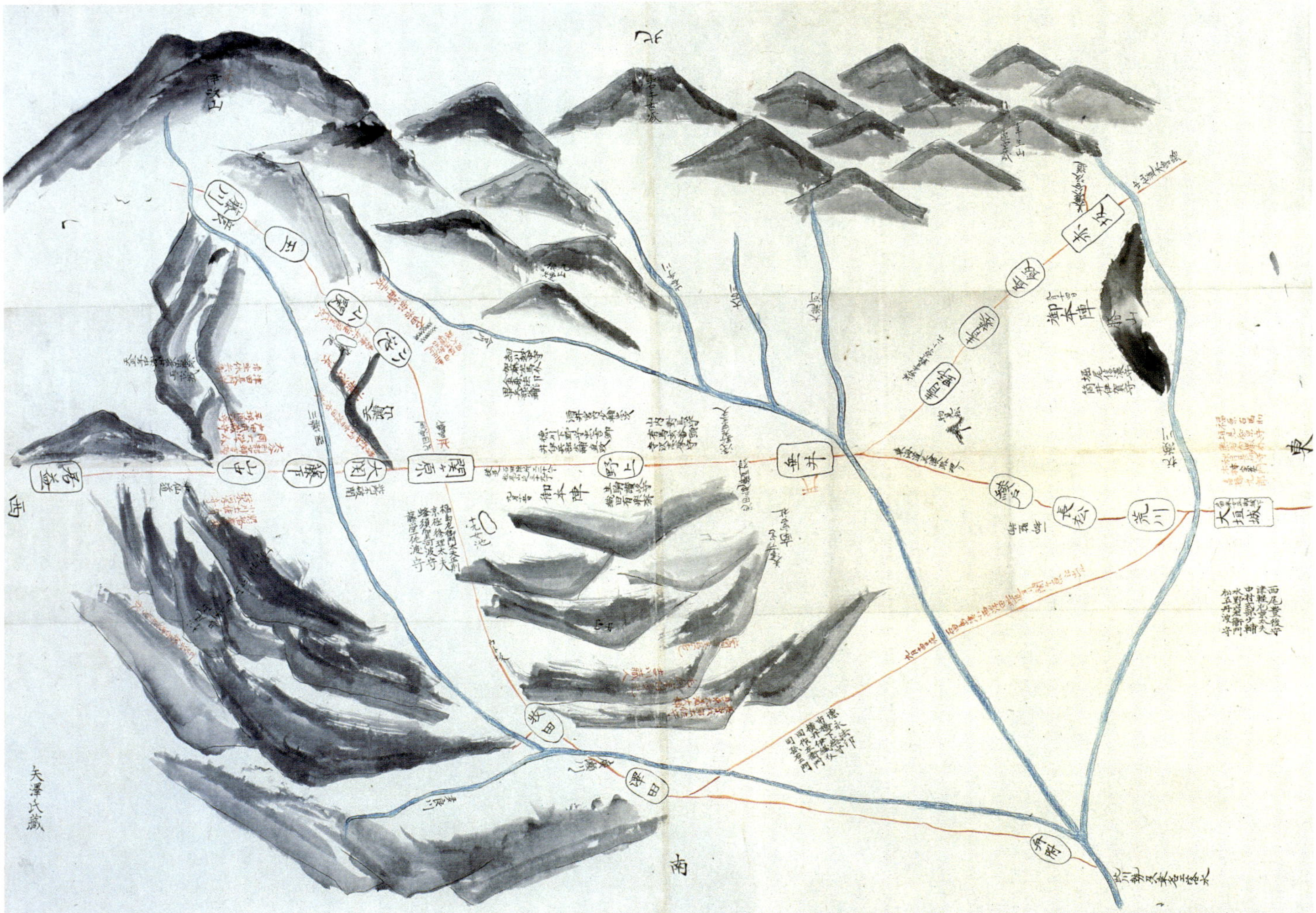

42 Sketch map (*kakemono*)

Illustrating the deployment of forces at the battle of Seki ga Hara

Edo period (1603 – 1867)

Ink and colour on paper

Association for the Advancement of Nagoya Castle

This sketch map illustrates the deployment of the forces of both the Western and Eastern Armies around the village of Seki ga Hara prior to the start of the battle. The map is drawn with Seki ga Hara to the left of centre at the junction of two roads drawn in red. The various blocks of text in red are units of the Western Army blocking the exits to the West, whilst the Eastern Army is shown in black. Tokugawa Ieyasu, flanked by Ii and Sakai forces, is shown advancing along the valley running east to west, while other units of the Eastern Army block the side valley from the south. Ishida Mitsunari is positioned between the two rivers running from the northwest.

In the illustration above, north is at the top.

43 | Portrait of Ishida Mitsunari

Dated 1900

Artist: Kishi Masaru
Ink and colours on paper
Ryotanji Temple

Ishida Mitsunari (1560? – 1600) was born at Ishida in Omi province and was recruited into the service of Toyotomi Hideyoshi around 1578. Although he did see some military action he was primarily an administrator, reporting to Toyotomi Hideyoshi on the performance of armies during the invasion of Korea and acting as one of the commissioners responsible for the administration of Japan during the minority of Toyotomi Hideyoshi's son. He was outspoken, tactless and something of a schemer, making many enemies of whom Tokugawa Ieyasu was one. In 1599 he was instrumental in plotting an assassination attempt on Tokugawa Ieyasu.

Although he acted as the focus for the Toyotomi supporters during the lead up to Seki ga Hara, many of the *daimyo* distrusted him or doubted his ability to command. Remembering former insults, some *daimyo* decided to change sides during the battle leading to Ishida Mitsunari's downfall. Following his defeat and flight, he was hunted down and captured a few days later. His father and brother, Masazumi, committed suicide whilst Ishida Mitsunari himself was taken to the Rokujo ga Hara execution grounds in Kyoto where he was beheaded.

This portrait of Ishida Mitsunari was commissioned to celebrate the 300th anniversary of Seki ga Hara. It is inscribed '*Kohun*', the name of the Head Priest of Tenryuji Temple in Kyoto, who conducted a memorial service for the war dead. It later passed into the possession of a direct descendant of Tanaka Yoshimasa, who had captured Ishida Mitsunari after the battle of Seki ga Hara. It was presented later to Ryotanji Temple, where there is a memorial to Ishida Mitsunari.

44 Portrait of Ishida Mitsunari

About 1970

Artist: Maeda Mikio
Ink and colour on silk

Nagahama Castle Historical Museum

This portrait is one of three painted by Maeda Mikio about 1970, the others being in Osaka Castle and the Daitoku-ji Temple in Kyoto. All three are based on photographs of the skull of Ishida Mitsunari that was exhumed from his grave in Daitoku-ji Temple during the early years of the 20th century.

The portrait differs from the previous one in showing Ishida Mitsunari as a warrior, with a dirk and wearing a formal costume called *kamishimo*.

45 Portrait of Ishida Mitsunari

About 1970

Artist: Maeda Mikio
Ink and colour on silk

Osaka Castle Museum

Details as above.

FROM SHOGUN TO DEITY

Oda Nobunaga pounded the rice
Toyotomi Hideyoshi baked the cakes
Tokugawa Ieyasu ate them

Japanese proverb

In 1603 the Emperor Go Yozei appointed Tokugawa Ieyasu shogun. This powerful position had originated centuries earlier when a warrior named Minamoto Yoritomo had obtained authority from the emperor to establish a military government. The title he had taken was the ancient one of '*Seii Taishogun*', or 'Barbarian-destroying Commander in Chief', generally abbreviated to Shogun. Since that time, the power to run the country had resided with the shogun and his military government.

46 | Folding screen (*byobu*) decorated with a map of the world

Mid 18th century

Wood, paper, lacquer, ink and colours

Hikone Castle Museum

Screens showing maps of the world or scenes of foreign countries became popular during the second half of the 16th century, as knowledge of the world became more wide spread in Japan after the arrival of the Europeans. These world maps were normally paired with a similar screen showing the geography of Japan. Tokugawa Ieyasu showed considerable interest in geography and received tuition in this, in navigation and similar subjects from William Adams. He also made attempts to establish personal relationships with the rulers of various countries, corresponding and exchanging gifts with the king of Thailand and sending gifts to European monarchs including King James I and VI, King Philip III of Spain and King Louis XIII of France.

This screen was commissioned by Higuchi Dosen, a vassal of the Tsugaru family, who occupied Sumpu Castle, and was copied from an original Chinese map dating from the Ming dynasty.

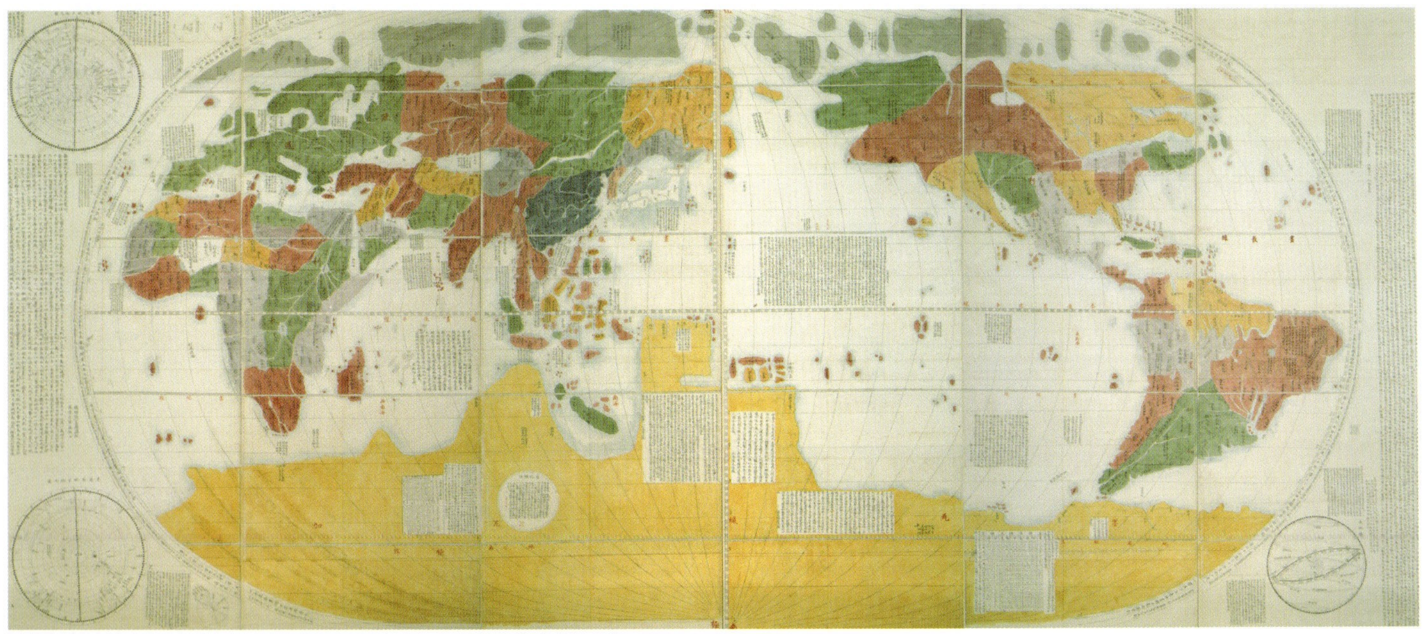

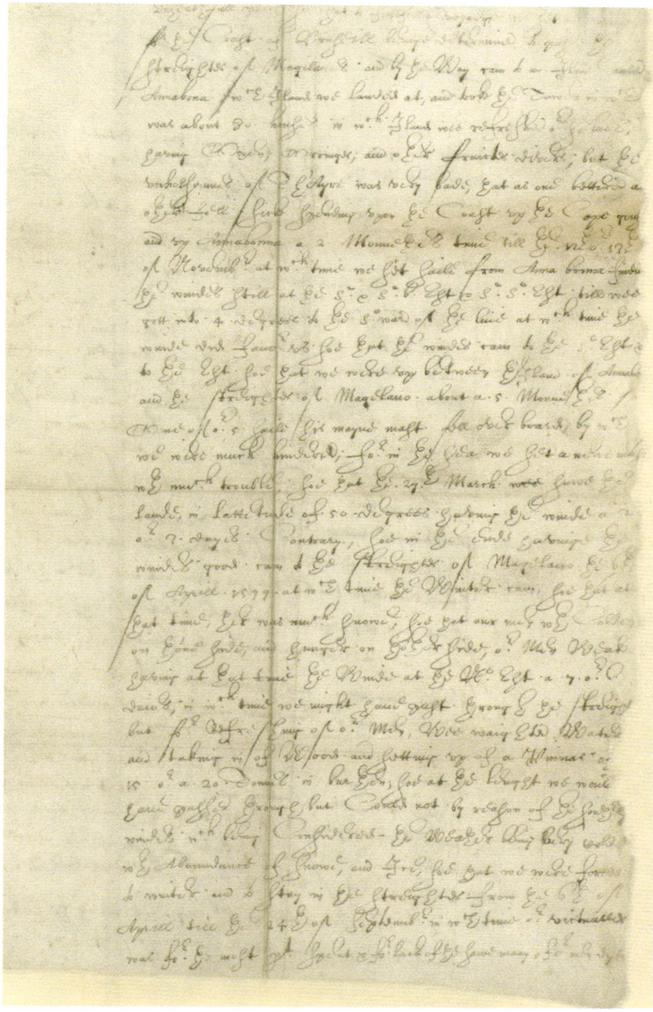

47 Letter of William Adams

Written in Japan in 1611

Ink on paper

British Library

William Adams was born in Gillingham, Kent and served on an English ship that sailed against the Spanish Armada. In 1598 he sailed as pilot-major of a fleet of five Dutch ships intending to trade in Spanish America. After trading in Peru Adams' ship was swept across the Pacific, making landfall on Kyushu. Despite numerous attempts by the Jesuits to have him executed as a pirate Tokugawa Ieyasu recognized his potential as a source of knowledge about such subjects as navigation and geography and eventually made him a vassal. Years later he learned of English traders in Java from a Dutch trade delegation and sent this letter to them, telling the story of how he reached Japan and his subsequent adventures.

The letter starts:

To my Unknown Friends and Countrymen
Having so good occasion, by hearing that certain English merchants lie in the island of Java, although by name unknown, I have emboldened myself to write these few lines, desiring the Worshipful Company being unknown to me, to pardon my stoutness. My reason that I do write, is first as conscience doth bind me with love to my countrymen and country. Your Worships, to whom this present writing shall come, is to give you to understand that I am a Kentish man, born in the town called Gillingham, two English miles from Rochester, one mile from Chatham, where the Kings ships do lie: ....

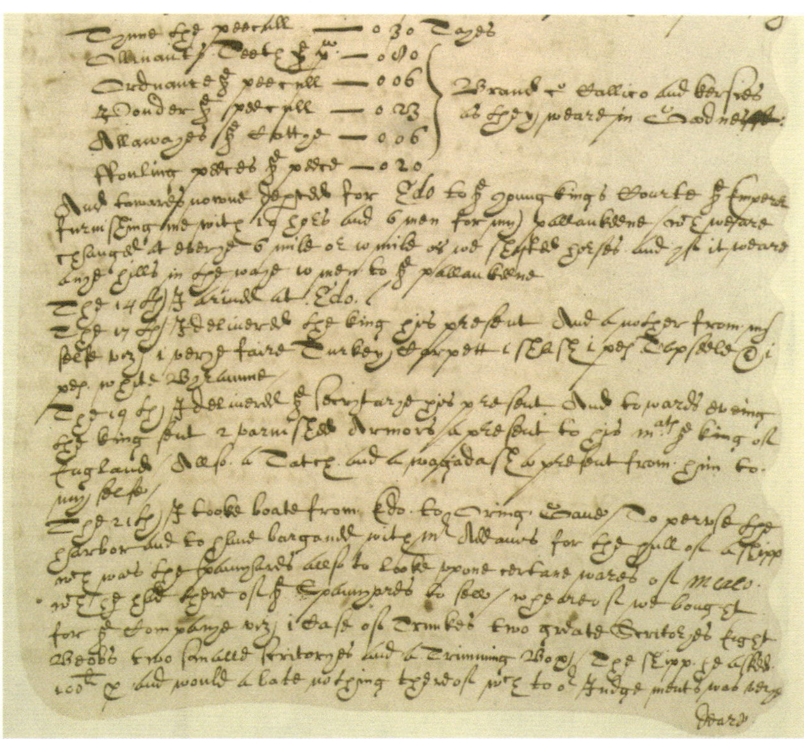

48 Diary of Captain John Saris

About 1613

Ink on paper

British Library

Captain John Saris was commissioned by the East India Company to sail to the East Indies with a flotilla of three ships to purchase a cargo of spices. His instructions stated that should he fail to obtain sufficient spices he was to send two ships back to England and sail on to Japan to negotiate a trading treaty. Saris kept a daily record of the journey for the benefit of the East India Company. In 1613 he landed on the island of Hirado off the coast of Kyushu. Tokugawa Ieyasu sent William Adams to meet him and escort him to Sumpu and subsequently to Edo where he met with Shogun Tokugawa Hidetada and presented him with gifts and a letter from King James I and VI. This page records the gifts of two armours and a sword for King James and a short sword given to Saris himself.

On the opposite leaf is a transcript by John Saris of the trading treaty drawn up by the Japanese authorities.

49 Armour (*do maru*), given to King James I and VI

About 1613

Armourer: Iwai Yosaemon
Iron, rawhide, lacquer, silk, leather and gilded copper

Royal Armouries XXVIA.1

In 1613 Captain John Saris in company with William Adams, the pilot of the Dutch ship *Liefde*, travelled from the island of Hirado to Edo, calling at Sumpu en route to meet Tokugawa Ieyasu. In Edo, Saris and Adams had an audience with the shogun, Tokugawa Hidetada, Tokugawa Ieyasu's son, and were granted permission to set up an English trading station in Japan. Saris presented Tokugawa Hidetada with gifts of cloth, silver and a gold-decorated gun. In return, Saris was presented with two armours, a sword (*tachi*) and a number of painted screens for King James, and a short sword for himself.

The two armours, like others presented to other European monarchs, were made by Tokugawa Ieyasu's personal armourer, Iwai Yosaemon of Nara. In total about a dozen of these diplomatic gift armours can be found in collections around Europe. The armour exhibited here is known to have been in the Tower of London since 1662 where it was described as Indian, a gift from 'The Great Mogull'.

50 Armillary sphere

Dated 1675

Manufacturer: Tsuda Tomomasa
Bronze, silver and gold

Nikko Toshogu Shrine

An armillary sphere is a skeletal framework representing the heavens that allows the user to predict star and planet positions. These instruments had their origins in the classical world, originally representing the Ptolemaic, Earth-centred view of the universe but were remodelled to represent the Sun-centred universe by Tycho Brahe in the 16th century. Large instruments were used for sightings, but this small example was made for demonstration purposes. At the centre is a sphere representing the Earth, the various rings representing the equator, the tropics and the ecliptic. Made in bronze, this was commissioned by Sakai Tadanao, *Daimyo* of Obama in Wakasa. The date scales use the Chinese zodiacal system in which the hours are represented by various animals. It is dated 1675 and is inscribed – an *'easy to use small celestial globe that was made by the gold, silver and copper artisan Tsuda Tomomasa'.*

51 Painting of a heron near water (*kakemono*)

Early 17th century

Artist: Tokugawa Ieyasu
Ink on paper

Kunozan Toshogu Shrine

This ink-on-paper drawing of a snowy heron standing near water was executed by Tokugawa Ieyasu. His use of empty space to give the impression of water and of distance shows a remarkably high level of artistry. It is not known who tutored Tokugawa Ieyasu in painting, but the style of the picture suggests that it was one of the Kano masters.

52 Certificate of appointment to the position of Shogun

Replica. Original dated 1603

Ink on paper

Nikko Toshogu Shrine

This certificate, issued on the 12th day of the 2nd month of 1603 on behalf of the Emperor Go Yozei, was the document that appointed Tokugawa Ieyasu to the position of *Seii Taishogun*. Having already set up his base in Edo, and built his castle there, this now became the seat of the shogunal court.

An approximate translation reads:

Councillor of State, Minamoto Ason (Tokugawa Ieyasu)
Official, Fujiwara Ason Mitsuhiro on behalf of the Emperor
Official, Fujiwara Ason Kanekatsu also on behalf of the Emperor
The Emperor has ordered that the person mentioned is appointed Seii Taishogun
1603, 2nd month, 12th day
Name and details of the issuing department

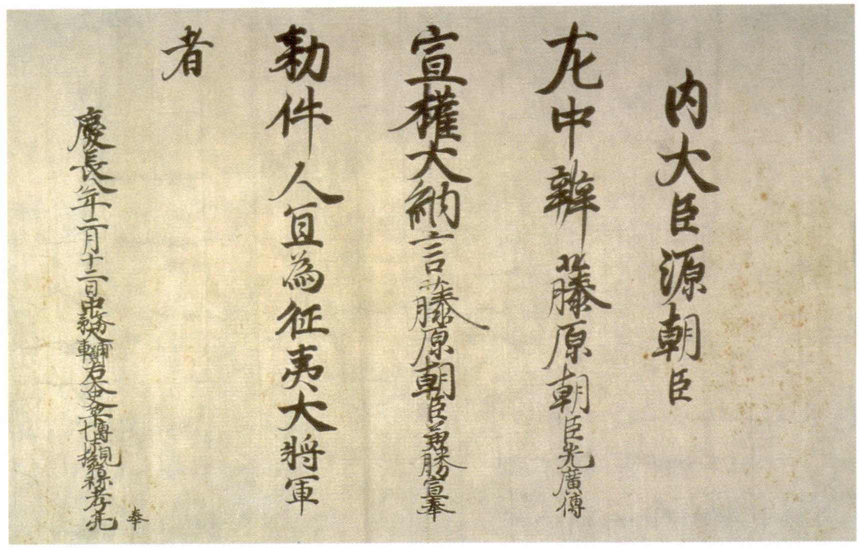

53 Certificate of appointment to the position of Prime Minister

Replica. Original dated 1616

Ink on paper

Nikko Toshogu Shrine

This certificate was issued by Emperor Go-Mizuno-o on the 17th day of the 3rd month while Tokugawa Ieyasu was on his sickbed. Its purpose was to appoint Tokugawa Ieyasu to the position of *Dajyodaijin*, a title that originated from the Nara period (646 – 794) conferring on the holder the right to administer the judiciary, the economics and politics of the country.

An approximate translation reads:

Government Official Minamoto Ason (Tokugawa Ieyasu)
Senior Official Fujiwara Ason Toshikatsu is instructed by the Emperor to notify the above that he has been appointed Dajyodaijin
1616, 3rd month, 17th day
Name and details of the issuing department

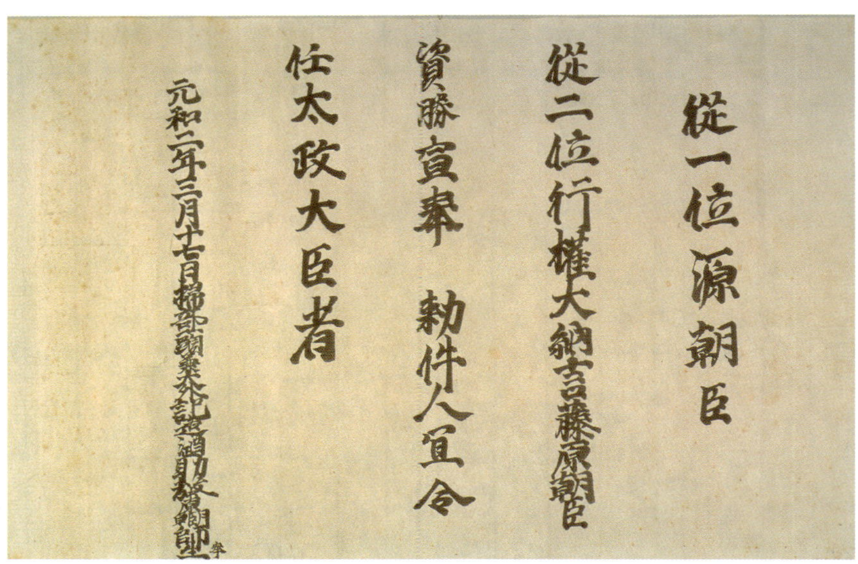

54 Folding screen (*byobu*) depicting the battle of Osaka Castle

Replica. Original Edo period (1603 – 1867)

Wood, lacquer, paper, ink and colours

Osaka Castle Museum

Winter campaign

By 1614 Toyotomi Hideyori, the son of Toyotomi Hideyoshi had gained his maturity and found himself becoming a focus for disaffected warriors, many being *ronin, samurai* who had been made masterless at Seki ga Hara and other battles. Anticipating a revolt, Tokugawa Ieyasu assembled some 200,000 men as well as hundreds of cannon and marched on the Toyotomi stronghold of Osaka Castle. Attracted by the opportunity of settling old scores, some 113,800 men assembled in Osaka to oppose the Tokugawa. After weeks of bombardment Tokugawa Ieyasu made offers of peace to Toyotomi Hideyori and his mother. By January it had been agreed that the Toyotomi would make no further moves against the Tokugawa and that the defences of the castle should be reduced.

Summer campaign

During the winter, Toyotomi Hideyori attempted to re-excavate the moats. In response Tokugawa Ieyasu renewed his offensive and marched on the now weakened castle. The defenders, realizing that the castle was no longer capable of withstanding another siege, harried the attackers on their march and finally met them face-to-face outside the castle. Although Tokugawa Ieyasu's army took casualties, the odds were against Toyotomi Hideyori who retreated into the main tower, set it alight and together with his mother committed suicide.

Winter campaign. (detail)

Winter campaign

Summer campaign

55 Calligraphic scroll (*kakemono*)

Early 17th century

Artist: Tokugawa Ieyasu
Ink on paper
Nikko Toshogu Shrine

This elegant calligraphy was written by Tokugawa Ieyasu himself. The characters read *kannin* (patience), a word that is also included in his Last Will and Testament. The scroll was presented to Nikko Toshogu Shrine by Matsumoto Ryojyun who was a doctor to the shogunate.

56 Calligraphic scroll (*kakemono*)

Dated 1616

Artist: Tokugawa Ieyasu
Ink on paper
Nikko Toshogu Shrine

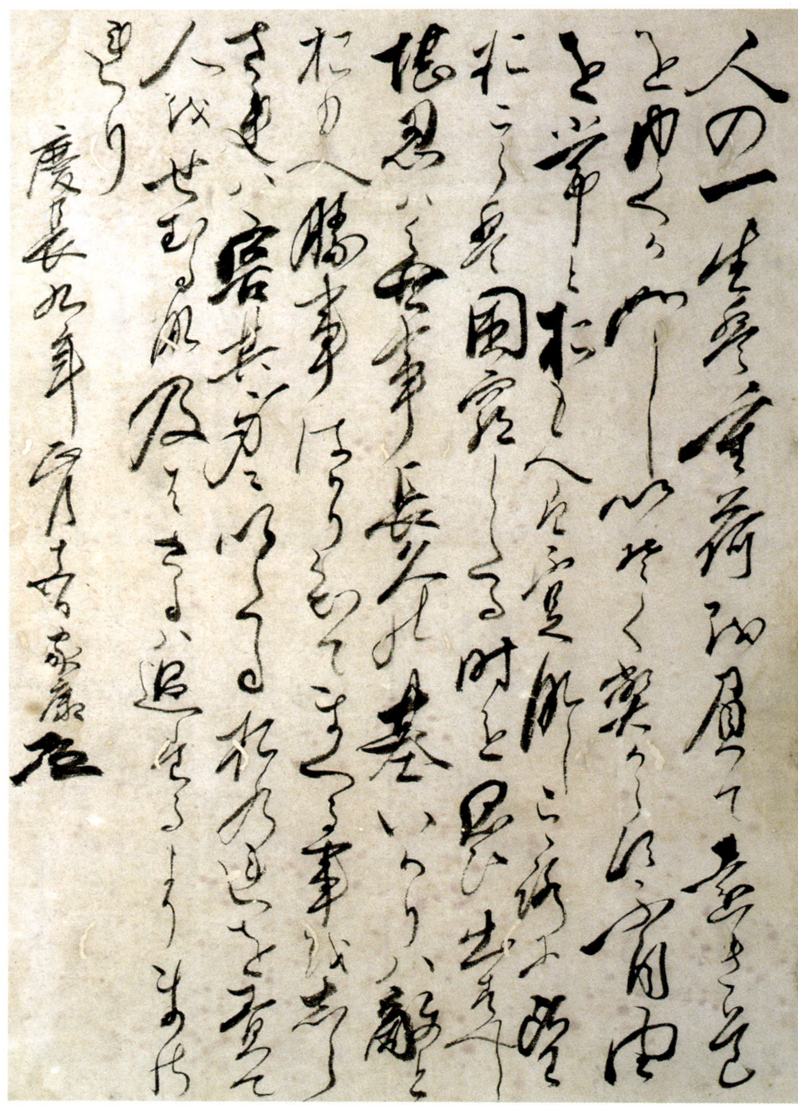

Although this is generally referred to as Tokugawa Ieyasu's Last Will and Testament, it is really a philosophical statement about life for the benefit of his descendants.

It can be loosely translated as:

A person's life is like going a long distance with a heavy burden on his back.

Do not make haste.

If you think of suffering as an ordinary state, you will never feel discontent.

If an ambitious desire seizes you, think of the days of hardship you have passed through.

Remember that forgiveness is the founder of eternal prosperity and anger is the enemy.

If you only know what it is to win and don't know what it is to lose, you will suffer the harmful effects of complacency.

Blame yourself not others.

Shortage is better than abundance.

57 Portrait of Lord Tokugawa Ieyasu

Early 17th century

Artist: Kano Sansetsu (1589 – 1651)
Ink and colours on silk

Nikko Toshogu Shrine

This formal portrait shows Tokugawa Ieyasu as the Shinto deity *Tosho Daigongen, or* 'Great Incarnation illuminating the East', a title awarded him by Emperor Go-Mizuno-o (reigned 1611 – 29). This title associates Tokugawa Ieyasu with the Shinto Sun Goddess, Amaterasu, and with the Buddhist Gongen, avatars who intercede on behalf of the living. The God is shown seated on a low dais wearing court robes and holding a slip of wood called a *shaku* on which was written the programme for a ceremony. The curtains which surround him are decorated with his hollyhock crest and before him stand two ceramic statues of lion dogs, *koma inu*, that still exist at Nikko Toshogu Shrine.

The artist Kano Sansetsu was born in the province of Hizen, the son of Senga Dogan. In about 1604 he moved to Kyoto to study under Kano Sanraku, marrying his daughter and being adopted into the Kano family. He eventually became head of the second generation of the Kyoto branch of the school, creating a style which used rather more detail than had been used by the first generation. In 1647, as the leading Kano artist of his day, he was awarded the title of Hokkyo, 'Bridge of the Law', the lowest of the ecclesiastical titles.

58 Handscroll, depicting the procession at the Toshogu festival

Replica. Original 17th century

Original artist: Kano Tsunenobu (1636 – 1713)
Ink and colours on paper

Nikko Toshogu Shrine

The highlight of the Spring and Autumn Grand festivals at the Nikko Toshogu Shrine, held on 18 May and 17 October each year, is the *Togyosai* or *Hyakumonozoroi Sennin Musha Gyoretsu* ('the hundred articles set thousand warrior parade'), which celebrates the transfer of the remains of Tokugawa Ieyasu from Kunozan to Nikko in 1617, a year after his death. The procession includes the portable shrines (*mikoshi*) of the deified Tokugawa Ieyasu himself, as well as those used by the spirits of Toyotomi Hideyoshi, deified by the Emperor Go Yozei in 1599 as *Hokoku Daimyojin* ('Great luminous deity of our bountiful country') and of the first shogun, Minamoto Yoritomo. Today some 1,200 parishioners take part in the procession wearing costumes of the early Edo period, including armours worn with the distinctive blue and white striped costume. Priests from the Shrine, and the sacred white horses, all feature in the processions. This handscroll shows how faithfully today's festivals mirror the original burial ceremony.

The original of this scroll was painted by Kano Tsunenobu, one of the foremost artists of the early Edo period. He was taught painting by his father, Naonobu, and after his father died in 1650 he was adopted by the foremost Kano school artist of the day, Kano Tan'yu (1602 – 74). He became a painter at the Tokugawa court, taking the tonsure and being appointed to the high rank of *Hoin* in 1709.

Armoured soldiers and spearmen

A sacred *mikoshi* being carried in procession

59 | Armour (*tosei gusoku*)

Early 17th century

Iron, lacquer, silk and hemp

Nikko Toshogu Shrine

This armour, one of a large number preserved at Nikko Toshogu Shrine, was originally used at the burial ceremony of Tokugawa Ieyasu and has been worn by participants in the annual festival every year since. The gold-lacquered helmets are of the type described as *zunari kabato*, or 'head shaped', a style popular around that period.

Most unusually the armours are provided with large shoulder guards, *o-sode*, rather than small shoulder guards. These large rectangular guards are normally used by people of higher rank. In the procession these armours are worn over a costume consisting of a jacket with tight sleeves and tight-fitting trousers, made of horizontally striped blue and white material.

60 Folding screens (*byobu*) of Genji Monogatari

Early 19th century

Artist: Itaya Keishu Hirotaka (1786 – 1831)
Wood, lacquer, paper, ink, colours and gold leaf

Nikko Toshogu Shrine

Itaya Keishu Hirotaka was an artist of the Sumiyoshi school which derived from the Tosa tradition of painting. He is known to have served the shogunate and was awarded the honorary title of *Hogen*. The subject of the screens, painted in an archaic style, is drawn from *The Tale of Genji*, a novel about court life written by Murasaki Shikibu during the 11th century. The two screens represent different chapters from the novel. One screen shows Prince Genji, wearing the court costume called *noshi* and a form of court cap called an *eboshi*, playing a musical instrument called a *koto*. He is joined by To-no-Chujyo, who is playing the flute, and Sa-Chuben who is beating time with a cypress fan. Other musicians are playing the *hichiriki*, a kind of flagolet and the *sho*, a small mouthorgan-like instrument. The mood of music is quiet, 'like the falling of a blossom', and a priest is shown listening.

The second screen shows Prince Genji dancing with To-no-Chujyo in the presence of the emperor. To the rear are two nobles dressed as palace guards armed with bows.

61 Lacquered sword box (*tachi hakko*)

Edo period (1603 – 1867)

Wood, lacquer, gold, mother-of-pearl, gilded copper and silk

Nikko Toshogu Shrine

This Edo period storage box was made to hold the sacred sword called *Tamamaki tachi*. The carcass of the box is wood, coated with fillers and multiple layers of lacquer, the top coats being coloured red with the pigment vermilion. Into this are embedded pieces of mother-of-pearl, further enhanced by clouds and the *kamon* of the Tokugawa family in gold lacquer. The original sword was lost in a fire during the 19th century when a storehouse at Nikko Toshogu Shrine was burnt down.

Particularly fine swords were stored in brocade bags that were then further protected by specially made boxes, that might themselves have their own protective bag and outer box of plain wood.

62 Lacquered sword box (*tachi hakko*)

Edo period (1603 – 1867)

Wood, lacquer, gold and silk

Nikko Toshogu Shrine

This Edo period sword storage box was made to hold the *Goho tachi*, the treasure sword of Tokugawa Ieyasu. The carcass of the box is wood decorated with *nashiji* lacquer. The box is further decorated with a design of peonies and arabesques in gold lacquer. The sword was lost in a fire that destroyed a storehouse at Nikko Toshogu Shrine during the 19th century.

61 ▸

62 ▸

63 Sword blade (*tachi*)

Early 19th century

Manufacturer: Fujiwara Kunimasa
Steel

Nikko Toshogu Shrine

This particular blade was made about 1800 by Kunimasa, a smith of the Edo Hojoji group working in Iyo province on the island of Shikoku. It was made as a replacement blade for the *Tamamaki tachi*. It was presented to the Shrine in 1843. Kunimasa was a pupil of Suishinshi Fujiwara Masahide who was largely responsible for a revival in sword making using blades made during the 13th and 14th centuries as models. The original sword was lost in a fire during the 19th century.

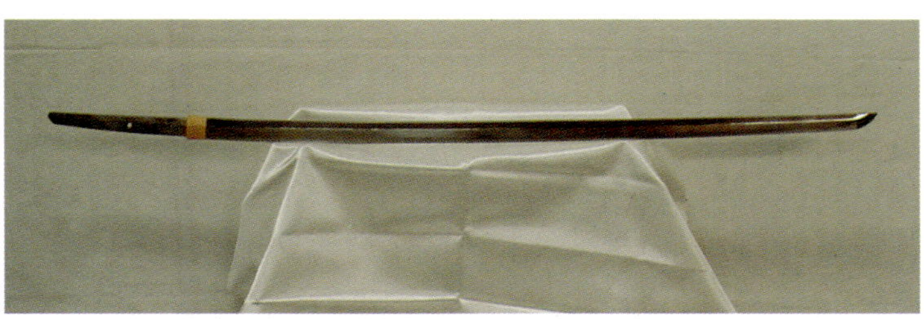

63 ▸

64 Sword blade (*tachi*)

Early 19th century

Unsigned but attributed to Fujiwara Kunimasa
Steel

Nikko Toshogu Shrine

This blade was also made by Kunimasa, as a replacement for the treasure sword *Goho tachi*. The original sword was lost in the fire that destroyed a storehouse at Nikko Toshogu Shrine in the early 19th century. The original *tachi* was stored in the sword box above (62).

64 ▸

65 Costume box (*awase hakko*)

Edo period (1603 – 1867)

Wood, lacquer, gold and silk

Nikko Toshogu Shrine

This box is designed for the storage of lined garments such as *kimono*. The carcass is of cypress wood coated with lacquer and finished with a *nashiji* ground in which flakes of gold are scattered throughout several layers of transparent orange/brown lacquer. Superimposed is a formal stylized design of scrolling tendrils in gold lacquer, known as *karakusa* ('Chinese grass', derived from a low-growing bamboo grass).

Four such boxes are preserved at Nikko Toshogu Shrine, the others being decorated with peonies, the Tokugawa *kamon* and a design of flowers and tendrils in a lozenge pattern.

66 Costume chest (*kara bitsu*)

Edo period (1603 – 1867)

Wood, lacquer, gold, gilded copper and silk

Nikko Toshogu Shrine

This style of storage chest derives from Chinese originals and is characterized by having legs attached to the side faces rather than to the corners. It is made of lacquered wood with mounts of copper gilt worked with a design of peonies. The tying cord is of silk. This chest is finished with a lacquer technique called *nashiji*, likened to the surface of a cut pear, achieved by sprinkling flakes of gold onto multiple layers of transparent orange/brown lacquer. Superimposed on this surface is a random design of the Tokugawa *kamon* in shades of gold lacquer.

This chest is one of a set of five similar boxes at Nikko Toshogu Shrine designed to hold costumes and accessories. It is dedicated for the use of Tokugawa Ieyasu in the form of the deity *Tosho Daigongen*. The other four chests are dedicated to the deities Toyotomi Hideyoshi, Minamoto Yoritomo and a visiting God and Goddess.

67 Noh mask (*fushiki-zo*)
Edo period (1603 – 1867)

Polychromed wood

Hikone Castle Museum

Noh is Japan's oldest form of theatre, originating in the 14th century from an amalgamation of street entertainment and the dance dramas of agricultural and religious festivals. By the Muromachi period (1392 – 1568) *Noh* had acquired the patronage of the powerful military elite, developing into a sophisticated art form. Sumptuous costumes and exquisitely carved masks were lavished on favourite actors, the various styles and types soon acquiring a specific symbolism. Playwrights often interwove reality and myth into their repertoire of stories, real characters appearing unmasked while those from the supernatural or from fables wore character masks.

About 250 different types of mask are known but only about 60 are used with any regularity. These masks derive from earlier forms that were probably created for religious purposes. By the Muromachi period they had evolved into sophisticated carvings in cypress wood covered by a layer of gesso-like material on which the features are drawn. Those masks that represent women in particular embody a harmony of realism combined with an abstract quality that enabled a skilled actor to vary the apparent expression of the mask by altering the angle of the head and creating shadows over the features.

This example, known as *Fushiki-Zo,* represents a mature young woman with just a trace of a smile, with loose strands of hair falling across the high forehead. The original version of this mask exuded resin on the bridge of the nose and around the eyes giving the appearance of a tear. Later copies of the mask often incorporate these slight defects in the carving.

68 Noh mask (*waka-onna*)
Edo period (1603 – 1867)

Polychromed wood

Hikone Castle Museum

This mask, known as *Waka-Onna,* again represents a young woman but is distinguished by having a hairline that divides into three distinct sections. Two thick strands run horizontally across the upper forehead, three or four thin strands at the level of the temple and three strands that descend from the temple, the innermost strand being thicker than the other two. It was fashionable for Japanese noble women to shave their eyebrows and redraw them on their foreheads using cosmetics.

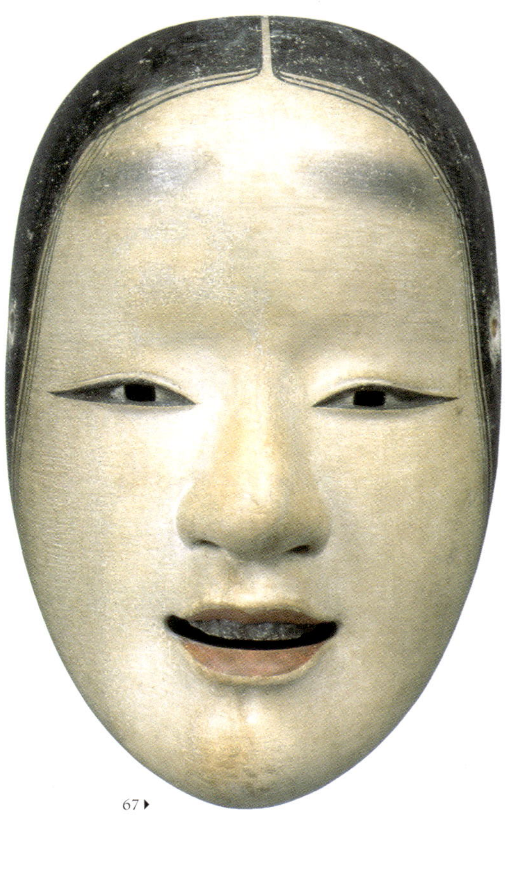

67 ▸

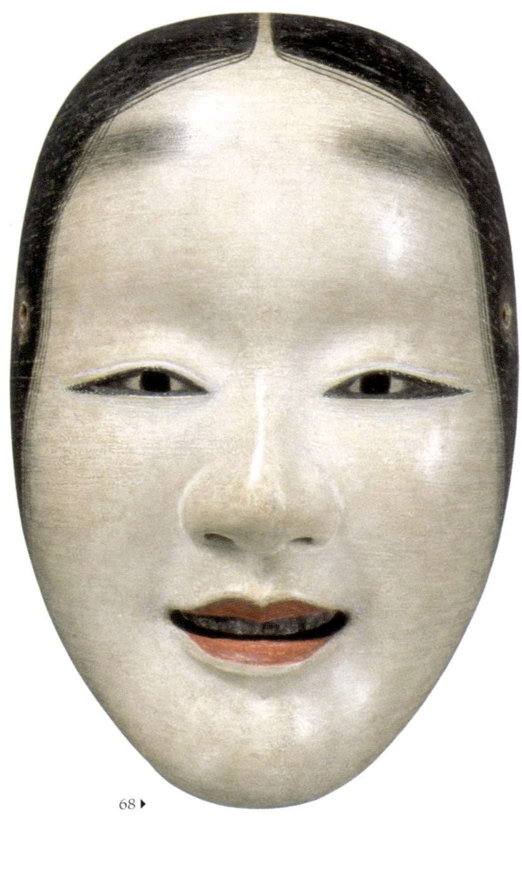

68 ▸

69 | Noh costume (*karaori*)

Edo period (1603 – 1867)

Silk and metallic thread

Hikone Castle Museum

There are two major categories of *Noh* costume; those with large sleeves having a wide wrist opening and those with smaller sleeves, as here. The term *karaori* means literally 'Chinese weave' and in *Noh* was usually worn as an outer garment by female characters. Quite often the basic brocade weave was augmented by embroidery in coloured silk or metallic thread. Those robes in which red predominates (*iro-iri*) were worn by actors playing the roles of young women, the red theme being echoed in such accessories as fans and linings. Those playing the roles of older women would wear robes in which red was absent.

70 Armour (*kawa tsutsumi do maru*)

18th century

Iron, rawhide, lacquer, leather, silk and gilded copper

Private Collection

Around the middle of the 18th century members of the warrior class, having no prospect of fighting, began to look back to the glories of their past. In an antiquarian movement, coincidently contemporary with the 'Gothic Revival' in Europe, armours and weapons were made that mimicked ancient examples preserved in shrines and temples.

This armour, of lamellar construction that wraps around the body and fastens under the right arm, was made for a member of the Oda family. It incorporates a wide-spreading neck guard and large shoulder guards that had been popular centuries earlier but had been abandoned during the civil wars as being too cumbersome. The entire cuirass is wrapped with a sheet of printed deerskin, a feature that had been popular during the 14th and 15th centuries as a method of keeping the lacing dry and protecting it from infestation by vermin. Here it is used solely for its decorative effect. A very similar armour preserved in Japan, also made for the Oda family, is wrapped in the same leather suggesting it may have been a family fashion.

Accompanying the armour is a document, drawn up in 1974, stating that the armour was made for Nobuhisa, Lord of Omi, the fifth generation from the second son of Oda Nobunaga.

71 Armour (*tosei gusoku*) decorated with Dutch leather

About 1750

Helmet by Saotome Ietada
Iron, rawhide, lacquer, leather, silk and hemp

Private Collection

One of the products imported into Japan by the Dutch was embossed decorated leather. In its homeland the leather was used for covering furniture and, stretched on frames, for covering walls. In Japan it was used for covering boxes, sword scabbards, horse harness and similar purposes.

This armour, made in the province of Kaga about 1750, has the front plate of the iron cuirass covered with a piece of Dutch leather that has been cut from the centre of a much larger panel. A mould for producing leather of this pattern, that depicts an acanthus plant amid rococo scrolls, is preserved in the Rijksmuseum, Amsterdam. The helmet bowl is by Saotome Ietada, who worked during the early 17th century, and it has been recycled from an earlier armour.

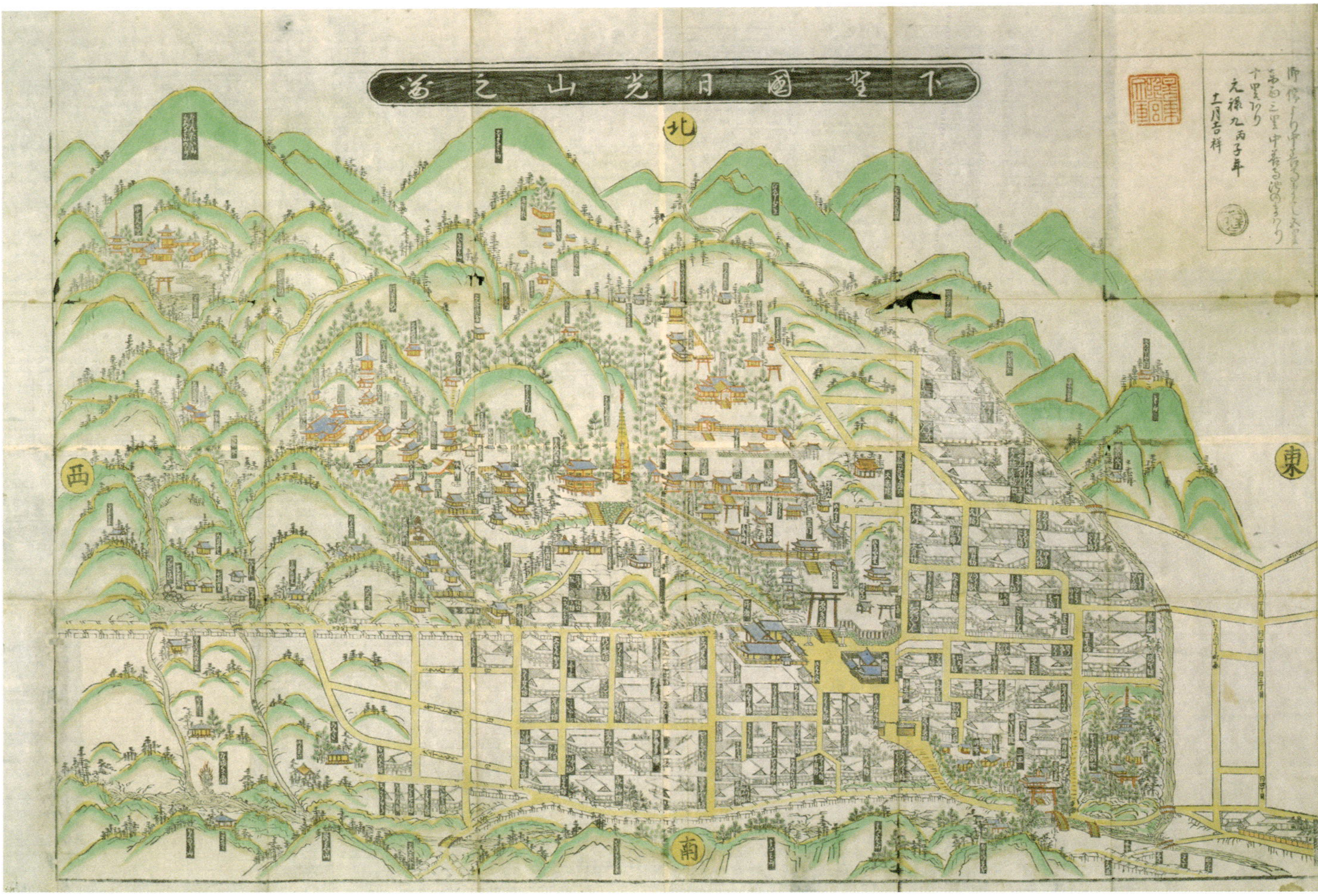

72 Map of the sacred precincts of Nikko Sannai (*Kaya Koku Nikko Yamae zu*)

Dated 1696

Printed paper

Nikko Toshogu Shrine

This detailed map of the Sannai area above Nikko town was printed in 1696. It illustrates the shrines and temples of the area in great detail, with captions describing each building. Nikko Toshogu Shrine is placed centrally with the great Ishidori *torii*, or gateway and the original five storey pagoda, the Gojunoto, marking the entrance to the shrine. Below this is the broad road past the Rinnoji temple where the *Hyakumonozoroi Sennin Musha Gyoretsu* procession makes its way down the hill during the Nikko Toshogu Shrine's Spring and Autumn Grand Festivals.

73 Map of the sacred precincts of Nikko Sannai (*Nikko Go-yamae ezu*)

Edo period (1603 – 1867)

Printed paper

Nikko Toshogu Shrine

The sacred area of Nikko known as Sannai, is above the town itself, in the hills above the river Daiya. At the centre of the area is the Nikko Toshogu Shrine. It can be distinquished as the complex of buildings above the great shrine gateway, the *torii*, visible near the centre of the map. To the west of Nikko Toshogu is the ancient Futarasan shrine. Below the *torii* of the Toshogu shrine is the Rinnoji temple, just above the Shinkyo Sacred Bridge over the river. All the hills above are covered with cedar trees that lend the whole area a peaceful atmosphere. This map was printed in Ueyama. The directions north, east, south and west are marked on as cardinal points, with north at the top.

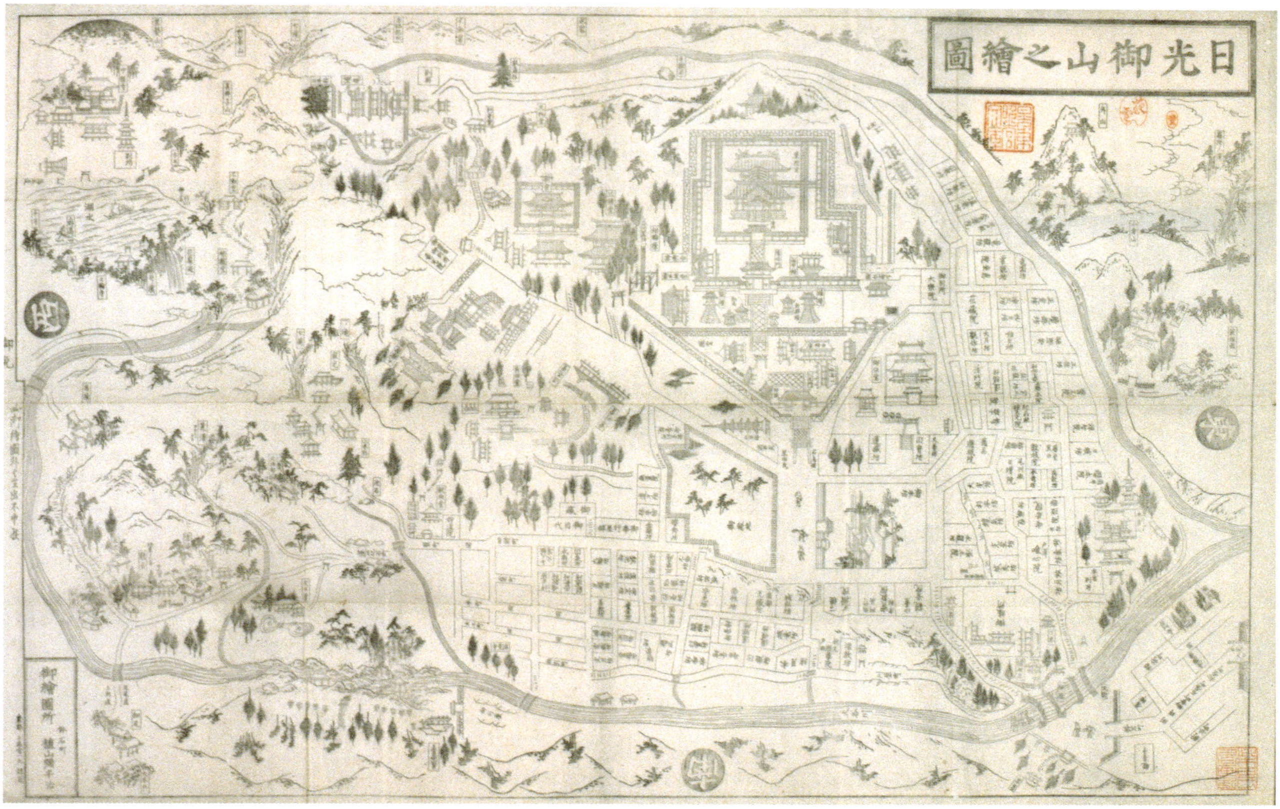

73 ▸

74 | Books on the topography of Nikko (*Nikko Yamashi*)

19th century

Author: Ueda Moshin
Printed paper and colours
Nikko Toshogu Shrine

This set of ten books describing the topography of the whole of the Nikko area were written by Ueda Moshin. They were presented to Tokugawa Ienari, the 11th Tokugawa shogun on the occasion of his visit to Nikko to pray to his ancestor in 1824. They depict examples of wildlife and plants as well as the mountain structures and the shrines and the temples of the area.

Map of Edo

Dated 1805

Printed paper and colours

Private Collection

During the early Edo period, the publication of maps of the capital was forbidden, for reasons of security, but it was allowed later. The frequent fires in the city, that destroyed whole neighbourhoods, demanded constant revisions. This map shows the shogun's castle, left deliberately blank for security reasons, surrounded by the mansions of the *fudai daimyo*, the 'inside' or trusted lords, within the outer defences. The position of each residence is indicated by the *daimyo's kamon*, or crest. The *tozama daimyo*, or 'outside lords', had to locate their residences beyond the outer walls. The map is orientated with west at the top.

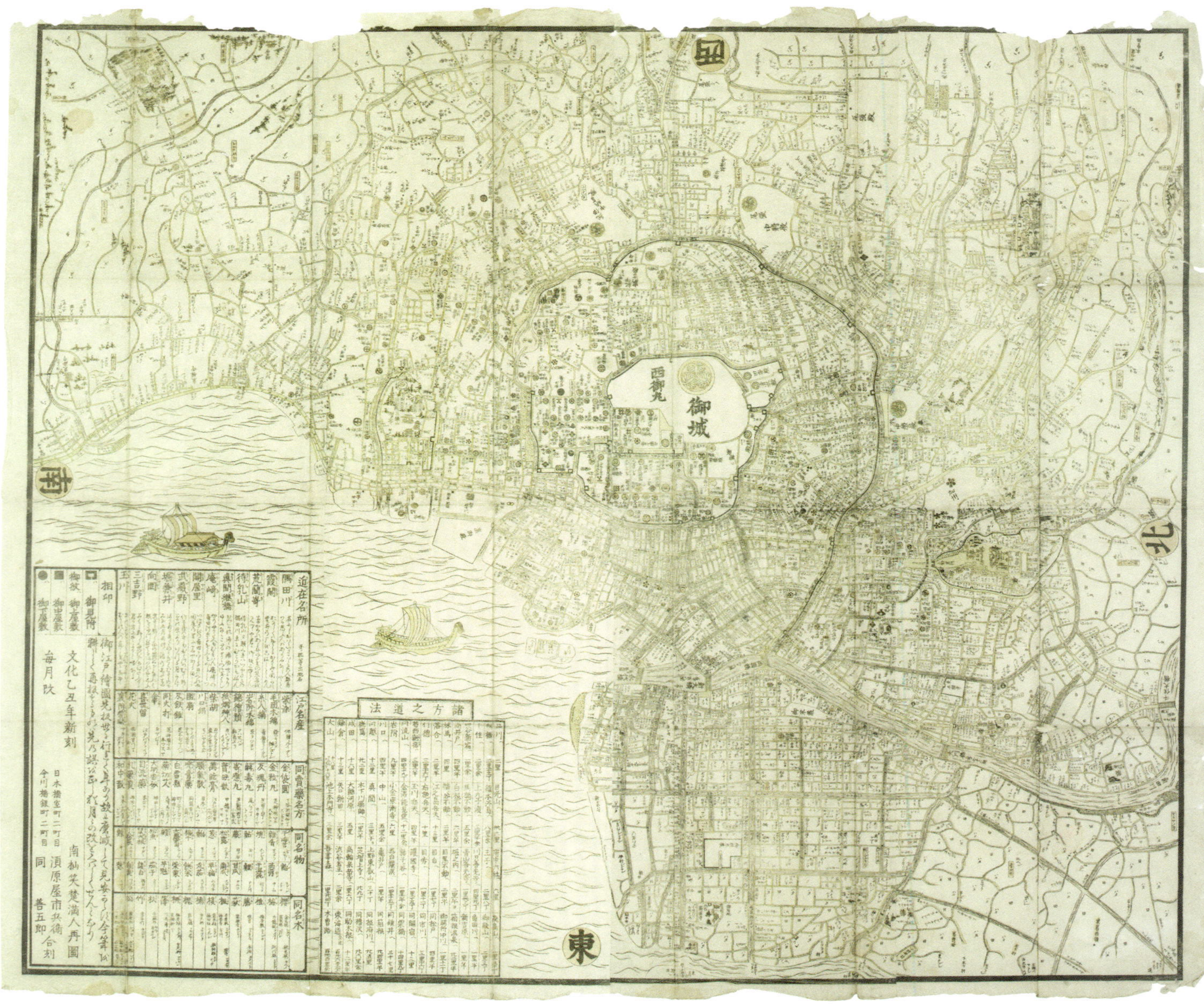

76 | Woodblock print of a daimyo procession

19th century

Ink and colour on paper

Blackburn Museum

The subject of this print is Otsu on the Tokaido road and shows part of a *daimyo's* procession entering the town. The main character, flanked by his *samurai* retainers, wears an elaborate surcoat or *jinbaori*. Most of the retainers are looking at a group of peasants kneeling alongside the road, probably to ensure they are showing the proper respect. Note the tall spears, one with a tiger skin covered scabbard, that were used to indicate the *daimyo's* identity.

77 Portraits of famous poets

Replicas. Originals early 17th century

Original artists: Tosa Mitsuoki and Emperor Go-Mizuno-o
Ink and colours on paper
Nikko Toshogu Shrine

These are replicas of six of the portraits of the 36 famous poets hung in the *Haiden* (worship hall) of the Nikko Toshogu Shrine. The original portraits with their calligraphy are national treasures and are not allowed to leave the country. The portraits were painted by the artist Tosa Mitsuoki and the calligraphy of their *waka* poems by the Emperor Go-Mizuno-o. Each *waka* poem is composed of 31 syllables in five lines, with 5-7-5-7-7 syllables. It is longer than the *haiku*, the other famous verse form of Japan, which has three lines of 17 syllables, 5-7-5. The more modern term *tanka* is a different way of reading the same characters. The classical poets illustrated in this selection are the male poets Kakinomoto no Hitomaro, Yamabe no Akahito and Ki no Tsurayuki. The female poets are Ono no Komachi, Nakatsukasa and Ko o Gimi.

Kakinomoto no Hitomaro was a courtier of the 7th century, about whom little is known other than his 19 long poems (*nagauta)* and 75 short *waka* in the *Man'yoshu*. He is regarded as one of Japan's most popular ancient poets.

Yamabe no Akahito lived in the 8th century, and is also known only by his surviving 13 *nagauta* and 37 *waka* in the *Man'yoshu*.

Ki no Tsurayuki, who lived about 872–945, was one of the compilers of an early anthology, the *Kokinshu*, and was a highly influential figure in Japanese poetry.

Ono no Komachi is perhaps the most famous female poet of Japan. She was a poetess of the 9th century, a woman of legendary beauty and passion. Her most famous *waka* were included in the first imperial anthology of about 900 poems, the *Kokinshu*. Only 18 of her poems survive, but they are regarded among the greatest of the genre.

From the 15th century the Tosa school were the official court painters. They worked in the style of *Yamato-e*, a colourful and realistic painting style used for narrative poems and novels, usually painted and written on sets of hand scrolls. With the decline of the imperial court during the wars of the 16th century the Tosa fell on hard times, but Tosa Mitsuyoshi (1539–1613) found a new audience for narrative paintings of Japan's classical past amongst the growing merchant class. He eventually moved to Sakai, the port south of Osaka to work. Tosa Mitsuoki (1617–91) was the son of Tosa Mitsumori and grandson of Tosa Mitsuyoshi. He grew up to become the last great artist of the Tosa school, and is known as one of the 'Three Brushes' along with Tosa Mitsunobu and Mitsunaga. As well as continuing and expanding the commercial commissions his father and grandfather had painted, he was appointed *edokoro azukari* ('Custodian of the Office of Painting') to the imperial court in Kyoto. It was his task in this post to record all the official events and ceremonies of the court, which continued despite the transfer of all real power to the Tokugawa shoguns. He expanded the repertoire of the Tosa artists into a Japanese version of Chinese *kachoga* ('bird and flower') painting, and his folding screens of 'quail, millet and foxtail' are among the finest early Edo paintings to survive.

The Emperor Go-Mizuno-o (1596–1680) ascended the throne as Japan's 108th Emperor in 1611. He married the daughter of the second Tokugawa shogun, Hidetada, in 1620, and became increasingly frustrated as power was taken from the imperial court to the shogunate. In 1629 he retired, handing the imperial office to his daughter who succeeded as Empress Meisho. He continued to play a role in affairs of state, being remembered for his cultural achievements, as a student of the arts and especially as the builder of the beautiful imperial villa, the Shugakuin, north east of Kyoto.

Kakinomoto no Hitomaro

Yamabe no Akahito

Ki no Tsurayuki

Nakatsukasa

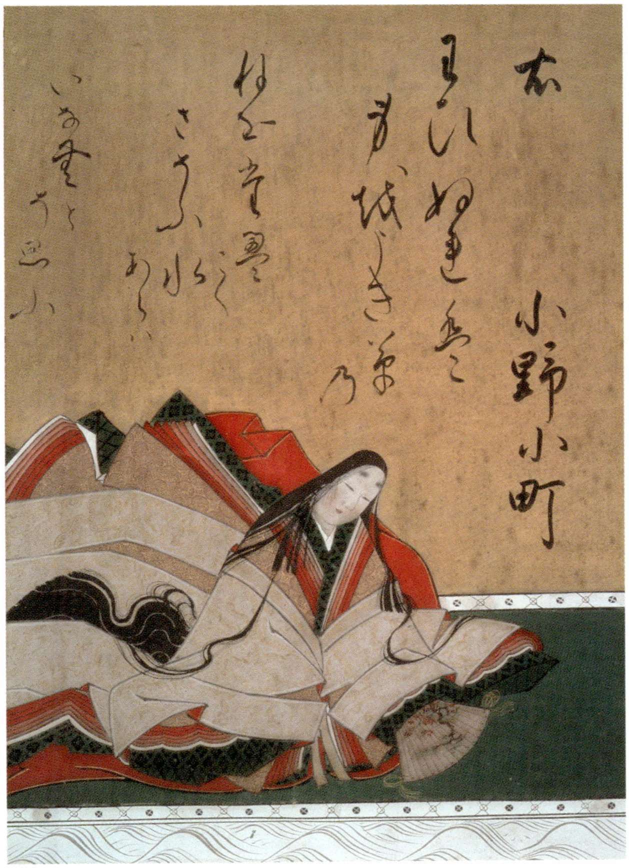

Ono no Komachi

Ko o Gimi

78 Set of books on the pedigrees of warrior families

Dated 1812

Artist: Hotta Masatoshi
Ink on paper

Nikko Toshogu Shrine

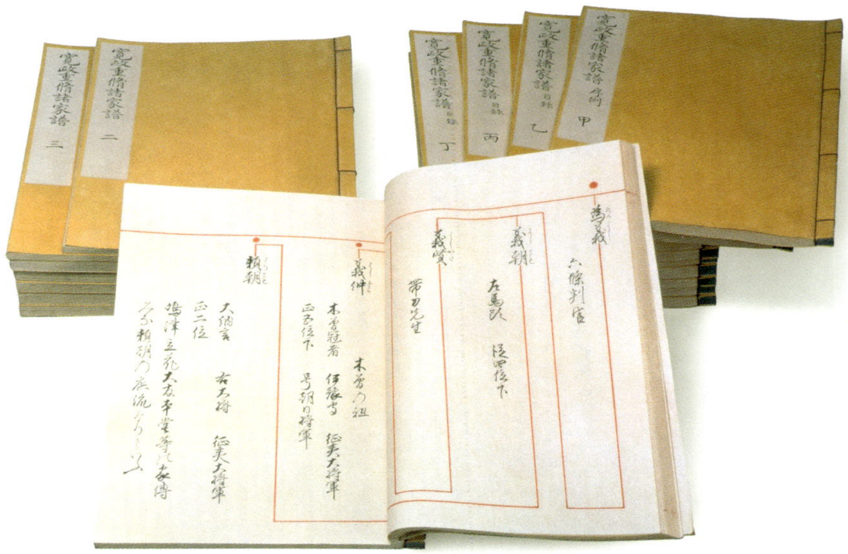

This set of books was ordered by the 11th Shogun, Tokugawa Ienari, from Hotta Masatoshi who held the rank of *Wakadoshiyori,* a secondary grade within the system of government set up by the Tokugawa. Exceptionally, Masatoshi had also been appointed to the office of *Tairo,* and acted as an intermediary between the shogun and his governing body.

The books took Masatoshi some fourteen years between 1799 and 1812 to complete, and contain the genealogies of all of the warrior families in Japan. Pedigree was considered very important in Japanese society and it was natural for the Tokugawa to want to record the ancestry of the *daimyo.* Only one other set of these books exist, preserved in the library of the Japanese Government.

79 Scrolls on the founding of Nikko

About 1640

Artist: Kano Tanyu
Ink, colours and gold on paper

Nikko Toshogu Shrine

This set of five scrolls were presented to Nikko Toshogu Shrine by Shogun Tokugawa Iemitsu in 1640 to commemorate the 25th anniversary of his grand-father's death. The set of scrolls depicts scenes from the life and subsequent deification of Tokugawa Ieyasu. More specifically they include scenes that show his birth, the battle of Seki ga Hara, his appointment as shogun, the summer Osaka campaign, his death, the construction of his shrine by his son Tokugawa Hidetada, the rebuilding of the shrine by Tokugawa Iemitsu and various beauty spots around Nikko Toshogu Shrine.

Kano Tanyu born in 1602, was the grandson of Kano Eitoku and begun working for the shogunate at the age of 16. In his early years he is known to have met Tokugawa Ieyasu at Sumpu. During his long career he painted screens and walls in Kyoto, Edo and Nagoya castles. This scroll is deliberately painted in the same archaic style, similar to the screens showing scenes from the *Genji Monogatari* (The Tale of Genji). Extracts from the scrolls have been used to illustrate pages 6, 10 – 11, 13, 15, 17, 18 – 19, 22 – 27 and 32.

61 朱漆塗り太刀箱

江戸時代
所蔵 : 日光東照宮

62 梨子地塗り太刀箱

江戸時代
所蔵 : 日光東照宮

63 太刀・銘藤原國正

作 : 藤原國正
江戸時代 : 1800年頃
所蔵 : 日光東照宮

64 太刀・無銘國正

作 : 藤原國正とされる
江戸時代 : 19世紀初期
所蔵 : 日光東照宮

65 衣装箱 (笹葉紋散蒔絵袷箱)

作 : 不明
江戸時代
所蔵 : 日光東照宮

66 衣装箱 (葵紋散蒔絵唐櫃)

作 : 不明
江戸時代
所蔵 : 日光東照宮

67 能面 (節木増)

作 : 宝生大夫重吉
江戸時代
所蔵 : 彦根城博物館

68 能面 (若 女)

作 : 河内家重
江戸時代
所蔵 : 彦根城博物館

69 能装束
(唐織 : 紅萌葱濃茶段青海波に色紙短冊菊萩文様)

江戸時代
所蔵 : 彦根城博物館

能装束 (唐織 : 金地枝垂桜に松皮菱散し文様)

明治時代
所蔵 : 彦根城博物館

70 甲冑

江戸時代 : 18世紀
個人蔵

71 甲冑

作 : 兜は早乙女家忠
江戸時代 : 1750年頃
個人蔵

72 地図 (日光御山之絵図)

筆 : 植山弥平次
江戸時代 (1696年)
所蔵 : 日光東照宮

73 地図 (下野國日光山之図)

筆 : 寺田重兵衛
江戸時代
所蔵 : 日光東照宮

74 地勢図集 (日光山志)

作 : 植田孟縉
江戸時代 : 19世紀
所蔵 : 日光東照宮

75 江戸の地図

江戸時代 (1805年)
個人蔵

76 木版画

大名行列
江戸時代 (1833年)
ブラックバーン博物館

77 歌仙図 (三十六歌仙勅額)

紀貫之・柿本人麿・山部赤人・
小野小町・中 務・小大君
原画 : 土佐光起 (1617～1691年)、
筆 : 後水尾天皇
江戸時代初期 (17世紀)
所蔵 : 日光東照宮

78 書籍 (寛政重修諸家譜)

国主・領主・幕臣などの家系図
作 : 堀田正敦
江戸時代 (1812年)
所蔵 : 日光東照宮

79 絵巻物 (東照社縁起絵巻)

徳川家康公の事績や日光山古来の縁起。
摸本
筆 : 住吉如慶・具慶
江戸時代 (1660年頃)
所蔵 : 日光東照宮

32 刀・銘備中次家
作 : 備中国住次家
鎌倉時代 : 1210 年頃
所蔵 : 日光東照宮

33 甲冑
安土桃山時代 : 1600 年頃
所蔵 : ロイヤル・アーマリーズ

34 甲冑
(朽葉糸威縫延二枚胴具足)
井伊家 11 代井伊直中着用
江戸時代 : 1800 年頃
所蔵 : 彦根城博物館

35 鞍と鐙
(黒漆塗葵紋菊蒔絵鞍・同鐙)
作 : 伊勢貞房
江戸時代 (1662 年)
所蔵 : 彦根城博物館

36 鞍と鐙
(黒塗葵紋菊蒔絵鞍・同鐙)
作 : 辻山城守政也
江戸時代 (1682 年)
所蔵 : 彦根城博物館

37 掛け軸 (家康と徳川十六将図)
徳川家康公と 16 人の家臣
筆 : 金村等徳
江戸時代
所蔵 : (財) 名古屋城振興協会

38 掛け軸 (徳川二十将図)
徳川家康公と 20 人の家臣
筆 : 狩野永納
江戸時代
所蔵 : 日光東照宮

39 弓道用手袋 (革製弽)
3 代将軍徳川家光ゆかりの品
江戸時代初期
所蔵 : 久能山東照宮

40 肩鎧
室町時代 : 1500 年頃
所蔵 : ロイヤル・アーマリーズ

41 絵巻物 (関ヶ原合戦図絵巻)
江戸時代 (1831 年)
所蔵 : (財) 名古屋城振興協会

42 掛け軸 (関ヶ原合戦布陣図)
江戸時代
所蔵 : (財) 名古屋城振興協会

43 掛け軸 (石田三成の肖像画)
筆 : 岸勝
明治時代 (1900 年)
所蔵 : 龍潭寺

44 掛け軸 (石田三成の肖像画)
筆 : 前田幹雄
昭和時代 : 1970 年頃
所蔵 : 市立長浜城歴史博物館

45 掛け軸 (石田三成の肖像画)
筆 : 前田幹雄
昭和時代 : 1970 年頃
所蔵 : 大阪城天守閣

46 絵図 (万国輿地図)
筆 : マテオ・リッチ (1552 ～ 1610 年)
江戸時代 : 18 世紀中頃
所蔵 : 彦根城博物館

47 ウィリアムス・アダムスの書簡
江戸時代 (1611 年)
所蔵 : 英国図書館

48 ジョン・サリス船長の日記
江戸時代 : 1613 年頃
所蔵 : 英国図書館

49 甲冑
ジェームス 1 世とジェームス 6 世への贈呈品
甲冑師 : 岩井与左衛門
江戸時代 : 1613 年頃
所蔵 : ロイヤル・アーマリーズ

50 天球儀 (渾天儀)
作 : 津田友正
江戸時代 (1675 年)
所蔵 : 日光東照宮

51 掛け軸 (水艸立鷺図)
筆 : 徳川家康公
江戸時代初期
所蔵 : 久能山東照宮

52 任命状 (征夷大将軍宣旨)
複製
筆 : 小槻孝亮
江戸時代初期 (慶長 8 年 : 1603 年)
所蔵 : 日光東照宮

53 任命状 (太政大臣宣旨)
筆 : 中原師生
江戸時代初期 (元和 2 年 : 1616 年)
所蔵 : 日光東照宮

54 屏風絵 (大坂夏の陣図)
複製
江戸時代
所蔵 : 大阪城天守閣

55 掛け軸 (堪忍)
筆 : 徳川家康公
江戸時代 : 17 世紀初期
所蔵 : 日光東照宮

56 掛け軸 (御遺訓)
筆 : 徳川家康公
江戸時代初期
所蔵 : 日光東照宮

57 掛け軸 (徳川家康公の肖像画)
筆 : 狩野山雪 (1590 ～ 1651 年)
江戸時代初期
所蔵 : 日光東照宮

58 絵巻物 (東照宮御祭礼絵巻)
筆 : 狩野常信 (1636 ～ 1713 年)
江戸時代 : 17 世紀
所蔵 : 日光東照宮

59 甲冑 (金塗装鎧兜)
江戸時代初期
所蔵 : 日光東照宮

60 屏風絵 (源氏物語図)
作 : 板谷桂舟広隆 (1786 ～ 1831 年)
江戸時代 : 18 世紀後半
所蔵 : 日光東照宮

1 屏風絵 (南蛮屏風)
筆 : 狩野孝信 (1571 ～ 1618 年)
江戸時代 : 16 世紀後半
所蔵 : 日光東照宮

2 掛け軸 (徳川家康公の肖像画)
筆 : 狩野了琢
江戸時代初期
所蔵 : 日光東照宮

3 木版画
作 : 安藤広重 (1797 ～ 1858 年)
江戸時代 (1833 年)
所蔵 : ブラックバーン博物館

4 旗
年代不詳
個人蔵

5 胸当て
18 世紀頃
個人蔵

6 折り畳み式甲冑
18 世紀頃
所蔵 : ロイヤル・アーマリーズ、個人蔵

7 折り畳み式兜
18 世紀頃
個人蔵

8 木版画本
雑兵物語 (兵卒の話)
作 : 春田信芳
江戸時代 : 1846 年発行
個人蔵

9 屏風絵 (長篠合戦図)
筆 : 不明
江戸時代
所蔵 : 大阪城天守閣

10 屏風絵 (小牧・長久手合戦図)
筆 : 不明
江戸時代
所蔵 : 大阪城天守閣

11 掛け軸 (豊臣秀吉の肖像画)
筆 : 藤原邦信
江戸時代 (享保 6 年 : 1721 年)
所蔵 : 名古屋市秀吉清正記念館

12 掛け軸 (豊臣秀吉の肖像画)
複製
江戸時代 : 1600 年頃
所蔵 : 大阪城天守閣

13 鞍 (菊桐文蒔絵鞍)
豊臣秀吉ゆかりの品
安土桃山時代 : 16 世紀後半
所蔵 : 大阪城天守閣

14 漆塗りの軍配 (桐文蒔絵軍配)
豊臣秀吉ゆかりの品
安土桃山時代 : 16 世紀後半
所蔵 : 大阪城天守閣

15 胸当て
室町時代 : 1500 年頃
個人蔵

16 胸当て (縹糸下散紅威胴丸)
豊臣秀吉ゆかりの品
安土桃山時代 : 16 世紀後半
所蔵 : 大阪城天守閣

17 掛け軸 (本多忠勝の肖像画)
筆 : 不明
江戸時代初期
所蔵 : 立坂神社

18 歴史集 (徳川実記)
徳川家の歴史
作 : 林述斎、成島司直
江戸時代 : 1843 年完成
所蔵 : 日光東照宮

19 屏風絵 (関ヶ原合戦図)
筆 : 狩野梅春 (複製)
江戸時代 (安政元年 : 1854 年頃)
所蔵 : 関ヶ原町歴史民俗資料館

20 兜 (角頭巾形兜)
江戸時代初期
所蔵 : 久能山東照宮

21 兜と面頬
江戸時代 : 16 世紀後半
所蔵 : ロイヤル・アーマリーズ

22 兜と面頬
作 : 春田派
兜は 16 世紀
個人蔵

23 大口径火縄銃 (大筒)
作 : 野田甚兵衛の銘入り
所蔵 : 関ヶ原町歴史民俗資料館

24 大口径火縄銃
江戸時代 (1603 ～ 1867 年)
鉄、銅合金、木
所蔵 : ロイヤル・アーマリーズ

25 火縄銃
作 : 江州・国友藤兵 (衛)
所蔵 : 市立長浜城歴史博物館

26 火縄銃
作 : 高倉甚六
所蔵 : 名古屋城管理事務所

27 掛け軸
(徳川家康と 2 人の武将の肖像画)
徳川家康・本多忠勝・井伊直孝
筆 : 小堀鞆音
昭和時代 : 1930 年頃
所蔵 : 日光東照宮

28 軍旗 (金扇馬標)
安土桃山時代 : 16 世紀後半
所蔵 : 久能山東照宮

29 刀取り付け具
16 世紀の型
所蔵 : ロイヤル・アーマリーズ

30 刀・銘藤原金道
作 : 伊賀守藤原金道
安土桃山時代 : 1590 年頃
所蔵 : 日光東照宮

31 なぎなた・銘備州長船景光
作 : 備中長船景光
鎌倉時代 : 1300 年頃
所蔵 : 日光東照宮

の家臣が行列に加わることもあった。平均的には約二千人で、百八十五人が直属の家臣、八百三十人が遠縁の家臣、六百八十六人が使用人や給仕、二百八十六人が馬手や雑用係であった。こういった行列には、加賀から三十二頭の馬が連れられ、百八十八頭の馬が各宿場町で調達された。

徳川政権下では、豊臣秀吉政権時に生まれた階級制度が体系化され、厳密に区分された。兵士階級の武家の身分が最も高く、次いで農民、そして芸術家や工芸人、商人は最も低い身分とされた。僧侶・医者・皮職人・同類の職人など階級は曖昧なものであった。構成されたグループの連帯責任と税の支払いは特に重要視され、その一員が責務を果たさなかった場合、グループ全体が罰せられた。徳川将軍家は大都市を統治し、全国に配置された大名が徳川幕府の指導のもと、各領地を統治に当たった。

家康公は概ね日本を訪ねた外国人には寛容で、ヨーロッパの国王との外交に積極的であった。しかし、秀忠公や特に孫の家光公の代になるとは次第に消極的になり、ポルトガルの政治的野心に疑念を抱くようになった。一六三八年、ポルトガル商人の交易活動を強制的に限定したのを機に、長崎湾の海上に出島と呼ばれる人口の島が築造された。翌年、オランダからも中国の絹の輸入が可能だとわかると、幕府はポルトガル人を追放し、オランダが代わって出島に進出した。当時の英国は、日本への輸出品が毛織物のみであったため、日本での交易の拠点を構えることを断念した。

日本の鎖国

数年にわたり外界との交流を閉ざす、鎖国の状態に日本は入った。渡航する大型船の造船や、国民が海外へ渡ることが一切禁止された。また、いったん日本を離れた者の帰国も禁じられた。鎖国下での唯一の例外として、オランダだけが出島での日本との交易を許可された。海外の情報や輸入品および将軍への貢ぎ物の提供をすることを条件に、日本はオランダに対して寛容な政策を取った。

鎖国によって徳川幕府は、これまでになく日本を安定した状態に保つことに成功した。芸術、特に町人による芸術が栄え最盛期を迎えた。織物・漆加工・鉄加工装飾・陶器・演劇・浮世絵などにおいて、当時世界で最も洗練された水準に達した。二百五十年間の徳川政権時代、日本はオランダからわずかな世界の情報を得るだけで、独自の発展を遂げた。稀な外国からの輸入品(たいていは将軍への貢物)は非常に喜ばれた。一七二五年、アラブから三頭の種馬が八代将軍徳川吉宗公の要求に応え将軍家に贈られ、西洋式の乗馬術も実演された。この三頭とその後に輸入された馬は、その後在来種と交配されていった。一七六〇年代には、オランダは電気機器や空気銃など、発達したヨーロッパの物理学や機械学の一端が紹介した。

徳川幕府の終焉

十九世紀初め、日本はオランダ人から、アメリカ人が太平洋を横断する米国の蒸気船を給炭する港を求めていることを伝え聞いた。この脅威は一八五三年マシュー・ペリー提督が率いる四隻の軍艦が江戸湾に来航して現実のものとなった。船上の大砲と最新の鉄砲で武装した米国海軍を目の当たりにして、日本はどうすることもできなかった。日本の鉄砲製造産業は、数世紀前、大名の鉄砲入手が禁止されて以来、実質的に終わっていたのだ。米国側の要求に応じ、開港する道しか選択肢はなかった。この後のわずか数年で、二百五十年もの間、絶対的な権力を誇った徳川幕府の幕藩体制は崩壊した。

反乱が起きたものの、十五代将軍慶喜公は朝廷に対し大政を奉還し、全国の大名は中央政府にその権力を譲渡した。徳川幕府は終焉を迎えたが、徳川家康公の伝説は未だに脈々と受け継がれている。家康公もまた日光東照宮から、関ヶ原の合戦で勝利したときと同様に、人々の行く末を見守っているのである。

た。また家康公はヨーロッパ人から大砲を大量に購入し、大阪城を砲撃した。攻撃開始から数週間後経っても、圧倒的な戦力を誇る徳川方にはほとんど被害が無かった。したがって家康公は講和を豊臣方に勧めた。秀頼とその母に申し出た条件とは、秀頼は大阪城に留まり、徳川方に対する反乱をこれ以上起こさなければ、徳川軍が撤退するというものであった。さらに大阪城の防壁も取り壊すという条件も加えられた。家康方は、反乱を抑えたとして、江戸に戻った。

豊臣陣営は、その冬の残りを城内で過ごした。春を迎えて豊臣方が堀を掘り始めると、この行動は講和協定に反するものだと家康公の怒りを買った。再び浪人やその他の反逆者たちが豊臣方を支援するとして再度結集した。今回、反乱軍は徳川軍が大阪に達する前に攻撃するという戦法をとり、僅かながらもこの策は功を奏した。しかし、豊臣軍の必死の抵抗にもかかわらず、家康公は大阪城外に兵を結集させて城を包囲した。豊臣秀頼は、弱体化した城に籠城しても、攻撃にはもはや対抗できないと判断し、城外に主戦の場を移すことを決断した。豊臣軍は果敢に戦ったが、徳川軍の圧倒的な武力差により、秀頼は城に退却し、本丸に火を放ち、母淀殿とともに自害して果てた。

神となった家康公

家康公は徳川家の安泰を確信された。日本の内戦は終わった。徳川家と本家に跡継ぎが生まれなかった場合にその跡継ぎを提供するために確立された尾張・紀伊・水戸の徳川御三家に反抗する勢力を持つ者はもはや誰もいない。一六一六年、家康公は病に伏した。後水尾天皇は病床の家康公に太政大臣の称号を与えた。太政大臣はヨーロッパでは首相に相当する位で、朝廷から日本の政治・司法・経済を司る実権が与えられた。一六一六年四月十七日、徳川一門の繁栄と日本国内の平和を維持するために、できることはすべてやり終えた家康公は、静かにその生涯を閉じた。

徳川家康公を祀る寺社

家康公は、静岡（正式には駿府）の久能山に埋葬されたが、その後、家康公の遺言に従って最終の安眠の地は日光に移された。江戸を中心に関東地方を守るため、日光が選ばれた。二代将軍秀忠公は正式に父家康公のために遺骸が運ばれた大谷川に近い丘に神社を建造された。後水尾天皇は、徳川家康公が東照大権現すなわち「東を照らす権現」になると宣言された。徳川家康公は国中から崇拝される神となられたのである。

それから二十年後の寛永十三年（一六三六）、東照宮の社殿は家康公の孫三代将軍家光公（一六〇四～五一）によって再建された。この改築には、四百五十四万人が昼夜を徹して従事し、完成までに約一年半を要した。造営費は五十六万八千両の小判および百貫の銀（今日の通貨に換算すると約二億ポンド）かかったと記録されている。東照宮の社殿は、当時最高の芸術家によって見事な装飾が施され、今日もほぼ変わらない状態で維持されている。一九九九年十二月、日光東照宮は世界遺産「日光の社寺」の一つとして登録された。

徳川家康公の政治

関ヶ原の戦いの直後、家康公は全国の大名を江戸に号令し江戸城周辺に屋敷を与えた。その後、三代将軍徳川家光の体制下で参勤交代が制度化され、大名は江戸と領地を一年ごとに在府・在国を義務付けられた。江戸滞在の期間と頻度は、譜代大名であるか外様大名であるか、また、江戸から各藩までの距離によってさまざまであった。江戸に半年の滞在を命ぜられる大名や、一年の滞在を命ぜられる大名がいた。各大名は江戸に居を構え、妻子を江戸に留め置かねばならなかった。江戸と各藩を往復する大名行列は徳川時代を特徴付けるものであった。領地の石高に応じて、大名は数千人以上に及ぶ家臣を引き連れなければならず、行列のための支度や、これらに従事する家臣に食事や宿泊場を提供したりすることは、意図されていたことだが、大名にとって経済的な圧迫となった。たとえば加賀藩の大名、前田家の場合は、外様大名で石高は百万石を超えていたため、三千人以上握されていた。一六一一年、家康公は後陽成天皇の退位式に出席するために五万人の兵を引き連れて京都上洛を果たした。京において家康公は御所の拡張を命じられ、また西日本の大名に対し、また翌年には、北日本の大名にも同様の誓いをさせた。

日本に到着した英国人商人

　同年の一六一一年、三隻の英国の貿易船が極東に向かった。司令官のジョン・セーリス船長は、三隻に万が一香辛料を満載できない場合は、日本に向かう命を受けていた。この年の後半、セーリス船長は香料諸島に到着したものの、満載できたのは二隻分だけであった。指示通りに、彼は荷を積んだ二隻を英国に戻し、自身はクローブ号で日本に向かい、一六一三年に平戸島に到着した。この知らせが駿府に届くと、家康公はウィリアム・アダムスを現地に派遣させ、セーリスを駿府そして将軍秀忠公と謁見させるために江戸まで同伴させた。セーリスの日記によると、彼とアダムスは折り合いが悪かったようだが、アダムスは将軍の代理人としての任務を忠実に務め、セーリスの献上品の選択に助言し、日本との外交儀礼の注意点を説明した。

　駿府に着くとセーリスは家康公に拝謁し、布・金装飾の鉄砲・銀食器、そして興味深いことに航海中に船大工に作らせた木のお椀を贈った。家康公とアダムスはセーリスに英国の交易の拠点を関東地方に築くことを勧めたが、彼は他のヨーロッパ諸国と同様に九州の利用を主張した。セーリスは江戸城で将軍徳川秀忠公と謁見し、布・鉄砲・銀食器などを贈呈した。しかし、これらは家康公へのものと比較すると明らかに劣るものであった。返礼としてセーリスは交易を許可され、また英国王ジェームス一世への贈り物として、家康公のお抱え甲冑師、岩井与左衛門作の二組の甲冑・刀・屏風絵などを与えられた。セーリス自身も短剣も受け取った。余談だが、これらの贈り物に関しては、ロンドンの東インド会社の者たちは屏風絵の質が英国王にふさわしくないとして、自分達の物と取り替えたという話が残されている。

ヨーロッパ君主と接触する家康公

　同年の一六一三年、日本はスペインに使者を遣わして、メキシコでの交易の許可を得、さらにスペインの交易の拠点を関東の北に移すよう、スペインを説得させるという決定がなされた。この任務を受けたのが、伊達政宗の比較的下級の家臣、支倉常長であった。家康公と将軍は常長にヨーロッパの主要人物への贈り物を与えられた。常長はルイス・ソテロ神父とともに、スペインの探検家セバスチャン・ビスカーノが遣わした船で、まずメキシコへ出帆し、途中ハバナ行きの船に乗り換えて、スペインに向かった。マドリッドで常長はフィリップ三世の御前で洗礼を受け、家康公から授かった甲冑などの贈り物を献上した。フランスと日本との交流はなかったが、家康が二組の甲冑をフランス王に贈ったという記録が残されている。これは、日本から贈られたとされる甲冑二組がフランス王家の収蔵コレクションの目録に記録されていることからも裏づけされており、現在もパリに保存されている。またピードモン公爵や、ローマ教皇と謁見するための船を常長のために手配したサボイ公爵にも甲冑や刀剣が贈られた。これらの献上品によって、家康公がヨーロッパの権力者との関係を築き、日本と世界との外交を強化しようとしていたことはまず間違いない。しかし、常長が一六二〇年に帰国したときには、この政策は覆されていた。

大阪城の包囲（大阪の陣）

　一六一四年になると家康公は、ヨーロッパ人・特にポルトガル人に対し政治的陰謀の疑念を持ち始めた。また彼は、成人した豊臣秀頼を今だ支持する者たちについても懸念した。秀頼支持者の動きが表面化すると、状況は悪化し、数千もの浪人（関ヶ原やその他の戦いで主君を失った侍）が、豊臣を支持するために大阪に集結した。

　日本最大規模の大阪城は、織田信長に取り壊された石山本願寺の跡地に建造されたものであったが、城の外周は約一三キロ・堀幅は三〇〇メートルあり、十一万三千八百人が滞在するのに充分であったため、豊臣の支持者が続々と集結した。家康公は十九万人を越える兵を召集し、大阪に向かっ

関ヶ原の合戦

石田三成は嵐の中、大垣から西軍を率いて、一六〇〇年九月十五日午前一時、関ヶ原に到着した。厳しい夜の嵐の中、上級武士たちは村の家々に泊まることができたが、下級兵士たちは急場を凌ぐ避難先を探さなければならなかった。ほどなく、他の西軍（石田三成方）も到着し、村周辺の丘や谷に布陣した。やがて悪天候・悪条件の中、夜が明けた。雨は降り止んだものの、谷は霧に覆われ、必死の思いで兵隊は食事を用意し、衣服や武器を乾かした。家康公は嵐が静まった午前三時に自軍の兵を動かしたが、これは西軍よりもやや状況が良くなっていただけに過ぎなかった。午前七時、泥や視界の悪さに邪魔され、東軍は戦陣を敷くのに手間取っていた。霧の中、「関ヶ原の合戦」として知られる小競り合いが始まった。

理論上は、谷からの道を遮断し、周囲の丘や山に兵を配置し、東軍を包囲していた三成方が俄然有利であったが、西軍の中には三成の意図や軍事指導者としての能力を疑う者が少なくなかったことを、彼は理解していなかった。特に、朝鮮での戦いで三成に批難された小早川秀秋は未だに恨みを抱いていた。その小早川は戦略上極めて重要な南の位置に陣陣っており、家康公には寝返りの意思を伝えていた。同様に三成に侮辱されていた毛利輝元も、三成のために戦うことに積極的ではなかった。輝元は背信するのではなく、陣地を離れず、できるだけ戦いに加わらないようにした。

ついに午前八時、東軍が兵を動かして、攻撃を開始した。同時に井伊直政と朱塗りの甲冑を身に付けた約三十人の兵が西軍の小分隊を攻撃し、その後、残りの兵とともに宇喜多秀家の陣を攻撃した。正午、東軍は小早川秀秋の寝返りを疑い始め、家康公は彼の決断を迫るため、丘の上の陣に向けて攻撃するよう命じた。せかさかされた小早川の一万六千の兵は山を駆け降り、西軍の大谷吉継を攻めた。この動きを見て、三成に対して不信を抱いていた脇坂・朽木・小川・赤座の各軍も寝返った。数で圧倒され絶望した大谷吉継は、討たれるよりも自害を選んだ。

短時間の内に、西軍の運命は確実な勝利から、敗戦必至に転じた。三成自身も戦いを止め、戦場から撤退した。午後二時になると、西軍では島津だけが、二百の兵にまで減少していたものの、孤軍奮闘していた。これ以上の戦いは無意味だとわかっていたが、降伏はしなかった。島津義弘は自軍に徳川家の陣に真正面から攻撃するように命じた。これには、甥の豊久が大将義弘の甲冑を着て義弘になりすまし敵中突破するという奇策を試み脱出したが、大勢には影響しなかった。毛利輝元と三万の兵は、自陣から離れず、実際に戦いに加わることなく撤退した。午後三時、戦いは終わり、東軍は戦場を完全に掌握した。自陣で腰を掛け、家康公は次のような有名な句を詠んだ。「勝って兜の緒を締めよ」。

関ヶ原の戦いが残したものは惨状だった。三万六千人が命を落とすか、重症を負った。敗走した大名は、捕われて殺され、家臣たちは浪人すなわち主人のいない侍となった。石田三成は戦いの数日後に捕われ、京都に連行され、刑場の六条ヶ原で斬首された。合計八十七の西軍の一族が根絶させられ、領地は没収された。

こうして名実共に徳川家康公は天下人となった。しかし、家康に反抗する勢力は依然残っていた。家康公はそういった大名の称号や土地を奪い、所有財産を減らし、更には、家を断絶させ、家康の家臣が監視する領地に転封させた。大名は、徳川直臣の親藩大名、関ヶ原の戦い以前から徳川に従った譜代大名、関ヶ原の戦い後に徳川に従った外様大名の三つのグループに分けられた。また、大名という称号が、年に一万石以上の石高をもつ領主のみに与えられることが初めて確立された。

将軍になった徳川家康

一六〇三年二月十二日、後陽成天皇は徳川家康を将軍に任じた。徳川家の本拠地、江戸の千代田城は将軍の居城となり、江戸に商人や工芸職人が集まるにつれて江戸は発展していった。家康公は将軍職をわずか二年で辞し、息子の秀忠（一五七九〜一六三二）に譲った。しかし、これは日本において特徴的なもので、引退後も大御所として日本の政治に君臨された。家康公は隠居先に、幼少期を過ごして慣れ親しんでいる駿府を選んだ。隠居して主に放鷹をして過ごしていたが、未だに国内において強大な実権を掌利輝元・宇喜多秀家・徳川家康公の五人に託した。また朝鮮から上記のような批判的な報告を送った石田三成を、内政を司る五奉行の一人に任命した。一五九九年に前田利家は死去し、代わりに徳川家康公が大阪城に入り、秀頼と他の後見人を仲介する最も重要な人物となった。

初の英国人の到着

地球の裏側では、一五八二年の四名から成る日本人少年使節団のことを忘れてはいなかった。英国商人は、日本との交易のため、北ルートでのアジア入りを何度も試みたが、北極海の氷によってその道は閉ざされていた。一六〇〇年になると東インド会社が設立され、アジアでの交易は正式に推進されることになった。

最初に日本に到着したオランダ人は、南米との交易のため出航した五隻の船団の中の一隻であった。ホーン岬を航海中に激しい嵐に遭って、船団は離れ離れになり、リーフデ号は南米のはるか沖に流された。数か月を要して必死の思いで太平洋を渡った生存者たちは、一六〇〇年三月、九州の豊後地方に漂着した。リーフデ号の操縦士はケント州ジリングハム出身で、エリザベス女王時代にスペイン無敵艦隊の撃退に加わったことのある英国人ウィリアム・アダムスであった。家康公はアダムスに会い、ヨーロッパの情報源として、またカトリック教国のポルトガルと宗教的対立関係にある点に非常に興味を持った。やがてアダムスは徳川家の家臣になり、ヨーロッパ人との会見に深くかかわるなど、家康公のために外交交渉を担当したが、彼自身は日本人の妻を娶り英国に戻ることは無かった。

日本の二極化

一六〇〇年、大阪城内の情勢は家康公にとって危険なものになっていった。石田三成による暗殺未遂の企てなど家康公に対する敵意が高まっていたのだ。家康公は大阪城からこの難を逃れ、自身の領地である江戸に戻った。家康公が強敵であると悟った石田三成は、若年の豊臣秀頼を守ることを口実に自身の支持者を集め始めた。三成が結成した連合軍は後に西軍と呼ばれるようになった。三成の行動を知った江戸の家康公は、東軍と呼ばれるようになる自身の連合軍を結成した。日本は東西二つに分かれ、両軍による戦いは必至となった。

初めに仕掛けたのは石田三成であったが、充分な策が練られていなかった。豊臣の後見人の一人である上杉景勝が三成方に付き、家康公が支配する関東の北部に大攻撃をしかけた。三成は、家康公を北の境界線に足止めさせられると確信し、西軍を日本の中央に結集させた。三成の指示を受け、上杉景勝は家康公を扇動させるために、次々に自国内に要塞を築き始めた。家康公は景勝の動きに、北の二大名、伊達政宗（一五六六～一六三六）と最上義光（一五四六～一六一四）を対峙させ、三成の動向を見守った。一方で、家康公は伏見城城主の鳥居元忠（一五三九～一六〇〇）に三成の西での動きを止めるように命じた。鳥居軍は果敢に抗戦したが、数で圧倒され、ついには降伏し、元忠は自害した。鳥居軍は三成の進行を十日間遅らせ、兵を三千にまで減らさせた。これ以上のことは誰も成し得なかったであろう。三成は美濃藩の岐阜城近くの大垣で、他の西軍が結集するのを待った。

九月一日、家康公がついに動いた。家康公は戦略上重要な岐阜城と清洲城が三成の手に落ちるのを嫌ったのだ。清洲は既に徳川軍側にあったが、岐阜はまだであったため、約一万六千人の先陣隊が清洲城の守りを強化し、岐阜城を奪うために送られた。家康公自身が到着するまでに、両城とも徳川軍のものとなっていた。戦況を見るために、三成は岐阜から約二五キロ離れた大垣に留まった。岐阜と清洲の両城を支配下に置いた家康公は、そこから約三〇キロほどしか離れていない東海道と中山道の主要街道も支配した。家康公はこの戦略上の重要地点を押さえたことで、三成より優位に立つことができた。三成は自軍の参謀の助言に反して、大阪の南の街道を封鎖するために兵を動かし、家康公を陽動することにした。三成が待ち伏せの地に選んだのは、大垣から約二〇キロ離れた中仙道と北国街道の重要な中継地にある、関ヶ原と呼ばれる山間の小さな村落であった。

て会見した。当然のことながら、秀吉は家康公に対して疑念を持っており、四国と九州を家康公と共に攻めるという申し出は丁重に断った。

一五八五年までには秀吉は国内の大部分を支配下に置いた。しかし、出自が良くなかったため、将軍の称号は与えられず、代わりに、朝廷は「天皇を補佐する者」という意味をもつ関白の称号を与えた。さらに秀吉は「繁栄している天皇の臣下」という意味の豊臣姓も与えられ、その後、秀吉はこの名で知られるようになった。豊臣秀吉は関東の相模・武蔵に注目するとすぐに、家康公に援軍を求め、一五九〇年、ついに豊臣・徳川連合軍は、権力者の北条家を平定するため小田原に出陣した。

古来より由緒ある家名である北条を名乗る武士の一族は、表面上は高貴さを装っていたが、実際は侵略や反逆を繰り返して領地を広げていた。約五万六千の兵を擁する北条氏の本拠地は、三ヶ月で約二十二万の兵の豊臣・徳川連合軍によって包囲された。激しい嵐などが連合軍には功を奏して、砦は崩れ、北条氏は降伏した。秀吉は家康公に、論功行賞で肥沃な北条氏旧領の関東八カ国を与え、家康公の領国（三河・遠江・駿河・信濃・甲斐）五カ国は織田信雄の所領とした。一五九〇年八月一日、家康公はついに領地を手放して、後に江戸、そして東京となる小さな漁村に本拠地を構えた。この関東転封は徳川家臣団の在地性が克服され、新しい領国支配体制を構築するきっかけとなった。肥沃な関東平野を治める家康公は 約百万石（一石は成人男子に必要な一年間分の米）を誇る非常に裕福な領主になった。

天下人となった関白豊臣秀吉は、武士と農民・商人・職人との身分を分け、全国を検地して土地と年貢の関係を一律に管理させた。流通経済の面でも合理化を図り、全国統一の法定通貨を鋳造させた。一五九五年頃になると、秀吉は戦うしか他の生き方を知らない武士たちの急増という問題に直面していた。従来は、同盟者や家臣には軍功として領地が与えられたが、もはや与える土地はほとんどなかった。代わりに秀吉は、報酬として優れた刀を与えることにし、さらに反乱の可能性を最小限に抑える改革を導入した。米の収穫高に応じて納める年貢を定め、刀狩令を発して武器を所有できる者を限定した。また、かつては武器を所有し、戦の際には馳せ参じていた小作人には、武士として家臣になるか、武器を捨てて農民としての生活をするかの、選択を迫り、監視員が国中を周って、農民からは武器を没収した。

秀吉の朝鮮侵略

さらに深刻さを増す問題もあった。特に九州では、キリスト教の洗礼を受けた日本人による紛争が起きていた。こういった問題を引き金に、また一方では、新たな領地を増やす必要に迫られ、一五九二年、秀吉は失職した武士に戦う場を与えることにした。しかし、それは日本国内ではなかった。秀吉は中国の征服を企て、そのために中国への通過地となる朝鮮をまず征服する計画を立てた。一五九二年から一五九三年の一回目の出兵には約十四万人が加わり、一五九七年から一五九八年の二回目の出兵には約十五万人が加わった。二回目の侵略時に、秀吉は朝鮮の近況を報告させるために側近の一人の石田三成（一五六〇～一六〇〇）を派遣した。三成は黒田孝高（一五四六～一六〇四）と小早川秀秋（一五七七～一六〇二）を、軽挙な行動をしたとして批難した。この報告が元で三成は後に痛いしっぺ返しを受けることになる。朝鮮侵略は戦略上の成功を収めたが、朝鮮の海軍に物資の供給を妨害されたため、侵略は継続できなかった。

日本船の多くが朝鮮遠征のための兵や食料や武器を運んでいた一方で、東南アジアに貿易に出ていた日本船もあった。これらの船は朱印船「赤い札をつけた船」と呼ばれ、幕府より正式な許可を受けて、安南・インドシナ・カンボジア・タイ・台湾・マライ・ルソンに渡り、日本からは特に刀剣や武器を輸出し、鹿皮・エイの皮・毛皮・象牙・香木などを輸入していた。主君のいない侍や浪人は日本での戦いの場を失くし、国を離れて、東南アジアの国々の権力者や、ヨーロッパの貿易会社の護衛を務めるようになった。特にタイの国王は、日本人の護衛を多数雇い、後には、日本人の山田長政を総督に任命したほどであった。

豊臣秀吉は二度目の朝鮮出兵中の一五九八年八月に死去した。秀吉は若い息子、秀頼（一五九三～一六一五）の後見役を、前田利家・上杉景勝・毛た。徳川勢は果敢に戦ったが、武田勢が徐々に徳川勢を圧倒していった。戦闘中、少なくとも二回は死の危機に直面した家康公は、ついに浜松への撤退を命じたが、全く予想もつかないことをやってのけた。彼は浜松城の門を閉ざすかわりに、門を開くよう命じ、逃げ戻ってくる家臣達の目印になるように松明を灯させたのである。この奇策は信玄を驚かせ、二の足を踏ませた。そのかがり火によって、城内には予想をはるかに超えた守備兵がいるように思われたのだ。信玄は大事をとり、夜が明けてから戦況を見極めるために一先ず兵を引いた。翌日未明、徳川家の小部隊が静かに城を出て、野営中の武田軍の本陣へ向かった。これは信玄の不安を掻き立てる行動であった。冬の季節になると、信玄は自分の本拠地である甲斐に戻り、家康公のもとから去っていった。

武田信玄はその翌年死去し、その後は彼の息子、野心家だがやや衝動的な武田勝頼（一五四六〜八二）が家督を継いだ。一五七五年五月、勝頼は父の遺志を達成させる時が来たとして、家康公の城のひとつである三河の長篠城を包囲した。再び、家康公と織田信長は武力を結集し、約三万八千の軍勢を編成した。一般に「長篠の合戦」として知られる戦いである。武田勝頼は城近くで戦うのではなく、名高い武田騎馬隊の実力を十分に発揮させるため、より広い場所を求めて軍勢を動かした。これを察知した同盟軍は、主力約三千の鉄砲隊を守るために川辺に杭を打って、迎え撃った。馬の勢いを止めるためである。押し寄せる武田軍は、水辺で馬の速度が落ちたところを次々に狙い撃ちにされ、この作戦の成功が決定的なものとなった。かつて無敵を誇った武田軍は、鉄砲による革新的な攻めの前には、なす術もなく打ち負かされた。武田勝頼自身は、生き残った家臣とともに甲斐山中へと落ち延びていった。

家康公と織田信長は、一五八二年五月までに合同で旧武田領を平定し、徳川家は駿河をその領地に加えた。この強力な同盟関係は順調に勢力を拡大させ、一方では、楽市楽座令の発布・関所の撤廃などによって領国内の経済発展をおおいにうながした。だがこの強力な同盟関係は、信長の家臣、明智光秀による、京都本能寺の変での信長襲撃により突然解消した。信長の最も有能な家臣として、百姓出身ながらも頭角を現していた羽柴秀吉は、即座に兵をまとめて主君の仇を討つため、直ちに京へ戻っていった。

ヨーロッパを訪れた日本人

徳川家康公と織田信長が日本の本州で勢力を拡大している間、九州ではポルトガル人との貿易が盛んに続けられていた。しかし東アジアのヨーロッパ人にとって、すべてが順調というわけではなかった。一五八〇年、ヨーロッパでの一つの事件が彼らに大きな衝撃を与えた。スペイン国王フィリップ二世がリスボン入りし、空位のポルトガル王の座に付いてしまったのだ。フィリップ二世がイベリア半島全域を支配したため、東アジアのポルトガル人の間には、フィリップ二世がスペインのために、ポルトガルの政治的支配権をスペインに移すかもしれないという恐れが沸き起こっていた。一五八二年、敬虔なカトリック信者のフィリップ二世に、イエズス会の布教が日本で成功していることを示すため、有馬、大村、大友の各大名家から、すでに洗礼を受けた四人の少年で構成される使節団がヨーロッパへ派遣された。羽柴秀吉は、絹貿易を維持するためにこの使節団が重要であることを理解していたので、フィリップ二世に対し、日本では君主間の贈り物とされた武器や甲冑を贈った。

徳川家康公と豊臣秀吉の同盟

明智光秀を討った後、羽柴秀吉は旧織田軍の指揮権を握ったが、これは家康公の怒りを買った。家康公は、織田軍の指揮は信長の息子の一人、織田信雄が執るべきであると主張した。この秀吉の暴挙に対して、家康公は一五八四年小牧に陣を張る秀吉を攻めるため尾張に軍を送り、小競り合いを繰り返した末、同年の長久手において最も激しい戦が繰り広げられた。小牧・長久手の戦いである。しかし、この戦いはただ単にに多くの犠牲者を出すばかりで、両軍にとって得るものはなかった。秀吉の軍統率力の高さを悟った家康公は、秀吉と戦うよりも、手を結んだほうが賢明だという結論に達した。和解のため家康公は翌年春、秀吉の本拠地の大阪城におい守護同士の対立が重なって、京の都全域を巻き込んだ長期にわたる市街戦が起こった。一般に「応仁の乱」として知られる戦いである。約十年後にその戦火が収まるころには、都の守護は軍勢の多くを失い、疲弊し、不安定な状態に陥った。何世紀もの間、権力を握ってきた守護たちは、自分の領地を取り返すために戦っては破れ、衰退していった。世にいう戦国時代、または「内乱の時代」の幕開けであった。この時代には、下層武士が、その主君を打ち滅ぼす下克上の嵐が吹き荒れた。

今川義元が立て直そうとしていたのは、こうした風潮を鎮めることのできない中央政府であった。義元が二万の軍勢を率いて、京に上洛を開始した頃、元康公は松平の家臣を率いて、丸根と呼ばれる小城を攻撃するため主力部隊からはずれて行動していた。大高城への敵方が兵糧を補給した翌日、敵の強い抵抗に遭いながらも、元康公は城を陥落させた。元康公がこの任務を果たしている間に、織田軍は、桶狭間に留まっている今川軍の本陣に奇襲をかけ、圧倒的な勝利を収めた。

元康公は、すでに勢力を失った今川家から離脱し、松平家の財政建て直しと、戦で荒れ果てた領地の回復を図った。一五六三年、彼は最終的に自分の名を、歴史上名高い「家康」に改名した。独立自尊の心の現れと見るべきである。また一五六六年十二月、彼は姓を松平から、一族の発祥地の名である徳川へ改名する許可を朝廷に願いでた。彼は自分の家系を調査して、新田一族へと遡り、更にはその新田一族を通して、鎌倉将軍家の源氏が先祖であることを突き止められた。

徳川家康公と織田信長の同盟

一五六一年、刷新した家臣団とともに、家康公は織田信長と同盟を結ぶ道を模索していた。一五六八年、信長が京都上洛を決定すると、彼とその家臣団は信長軍に合流した。しかし、家康公は、織田家との同盟で他との同盟の機会を失ったわけではなかった。甲斐と信濃の領主である、武田信玄は家康公が手を結んだ武将の一人であった。信玄は、軍の規模と戦闘能力においてその名をとどろかせた名将であり、特にその騎馬隊は名高く、それらを統率する本部隊も同様に優れていた。信玄は、中国古来の兵法を学び、その旗印には風林火山の文字を掲げていた。いわゆる、「速きこと風の如し、静かなること林の如し、侵略すること火の如し、動かざること山の如し」である。信玄が隣国との争いや宿敵上杉謙信との戦いに時間を費やしていなかったら、彼は日本の歴史にもっと偉大な足跡を残していたかもしれない。一五六八年、家康公と武田信玄は、今川家の旧領地を分割した。この新しい領土を得た家康公は、先祖伝来の地三河の岡崎城から、都と北部地域をつなぐ東海道沿いに位置する要所浜松城へと拠点を移した。

一五六八年、家康公と武田信玄が旧今川領の処理に追われていたころ、織田信長は将軍足利義昭を擁立して上洛を果たし京を支配下に置き、力を天下に誇示した。ついで信長は北陸への勢力拡大をねらったが、その行く手は比叡山延暦寺の僧兵によって阻まれていた。当時、寺内町と呼ばれる、世俗権力を離れた独立都市が寺院の敷地内に建設されたが、僧兵たちは、聖域としての特権という法の抜け道を利用し、数世紀にわたって軍事的・政治的な勢力を伸ばしていた。僧侶たちは巧妙な方法を考え出したのだ。それは、土地所有者に署名させて土地の権利を僧侶が譲り受け、無課税の恩恵を受けるというものだった。こうした利権を守るために、多くの寺では相当数の武器を所有した。信長は宗教への関心は薄く、軍事化した仏教徒を嫌って激しく対立した。一五七一年九月、信長はその情け容赦ない気性をあらわにして、比叡山を軍勢で包囲した。信長軍は合図とともに比叡山頂上への通路を駆け上り、寺社仏閣に火をかけ放っていった。

一五七二年十二月、織田信長の北への動きと家康公の浜松城への移動は、武田信玄の目には極めて挑発的なものに映った。機先を制するため、信玄は三万五千の軍勢を率いて、浜松へ通じる街道を行軍した。信玄のこの行動は、織田信長の耳元に即座に届き、信長は家康公に支援部隊を派遣し、警戒を怠らないようにとの指示を与えた。数において劣勢であるにもかかわらず、家康公は城を離れて、三方が原の浜松城の北方、武田軍にわずか数キロという距離まで接近した。一般に「三方ヶ原の合戦」として知られる戦いである。午後遅くなって、両軍は激突し、戦いは夜が更けるまで続い忠公の妻於大の方の兄）が織田家に味方したことがきっかけとなり、広忠公は妻を離縁して今川家に接近し、同盟を結ぶことになった。

家康公の登場

同盟の条件の一つは（当時全く当たり前のように行なわれてきたことだが）松平家が、嫡男である竹千代君を今川家の人質として駿府に預けるということだった。この同盟、および幼い竹千代君にとって不運な事に、この情報は漏れ、道中で一行は織田勢に待ち伏され、彼は尾張の古渡城に連れ去られた。今川家との同盟を破棄しなければ竹千代君を殺害するという織田信秀の脅しにもかかわらず、広忠公はこれを無視し続けた。その後、機会を得た今川義元は、織田方のとりで、安祥城に兵を送りその城の城主だった織田信秀の息子を捕えた。今川義元は織田方に人質の交換を申し入れ、幼い松平竹千代君の引き渡しを条件に、攻撃の中止と軍勢の撤退が行われた。こうして、約一年遅れて、竹千代君は駿府城にたどり着いた。駿府城では、竹千代君は高貴な客として丁重に扱われ、義元の政治顧問であった太原崇孚より最高水準の教育を受け、大名の嫡男としてふさわしい少年期過ごされた。

一五五五年の元服において、竹千代君は幼名を改めて松平元信と名乗り、後に元康と改名した。今川義元から授けられた「元」と彼自身の祖父、清康の「康」を合わせた名である。その後、元康公は松平軍の大将となり、彼と家臣団は今川軍の同盟軍として戦うこととなった。一五五八年、今川義元は十七歳の元康公に初陣として、今川家から織田家に寝返った鈴木重辰の居城の攻撃を命じたが、彼は家臣を失うことを避けるために、寺部城を火攻めした。結果、数日で四つの城が落とされ、全国に「元康」の名を轟かせることになった。

やがて、元康公と織田信長（一五三四～一五八二）の対立は避けられないものとなった。信長は、親族の強い反対を抑えて、父織田信秀の死後、尾張一帯を統治していた。また、実弟とも戦って自害へと追い込んでいた。

元康公と信長の衝突は、兵糧を切らしつつあった前哨地の大高城を、信長が包囲することに端を発した。若年にもかかわらず、元康公は織田軍へ直接攻撃することは無謀であると見抜いていた。元康公は包囲した城に敵が兵糧を送り込む時をねらって、攻める代わりに偽の情報を流し、信長が偽の情報につられて軍勢を移動させるように仕向けた。そして、信長とその軍勢の大半が城を出て行ったと見るや、松平軍は城内になだれ込み、実質的には無抵抗の大高城を落としたのであった。

織田軍は入念な下調べと迅速な行動で、松平領や今川領に侵攻を繰り返してはいたが、今川義元にとっては取るに足らないことであった。義元には、はるかに高い目標があった。一五六〇年までに、義元は松平家臣団を含む二万の軍勢を編成し、その勢いで天皇を擁立し、御所と幕府のあった京都への上洛の機会を窺がっていたのである。

戦国時代の起こり

日本の皇室は千年以上国を統治してきたが、殆どの期間、国政の実権は軍事支配者によって握られてきた。その政府のリーダーは、将軍、正確には日本の古代に起源を持つ征夷大将軍、すなわち「夷敵を打ち払う偉大なる将軍」であった。最初に軍事政権を築いたのは、十二世紀に現れた源頼朝であった。源頼朝公は徳川家の先祖として日光東照宮に祀られている。彼は御家人とともに他の有力な豪族を打ち負かし、天皇から政治的統治を任された。彼は幕府と呼ばれる軍事政権を鎌倉に設置し、地方の管理を地頭と呼ばれる土地管財人と警察機関である守護に委任した。十四世紀半ばには足利氏が新たな幕府を開き、幕府の権力は軍事・政治のあらゆる面にまで拡大していった。守護もまた権力を拡大し、地方における事実上の軍事政府として機能するまでになっていった。足利将軍家は、世代交代を重ねるうちに徐々にその力を失って、国を治めることよりも、京の都での快楽的生活に耽るようになっていった。同様に、辺鄙な田舎に住むよりも都での生活を好む守護も増えたため、国人と呼ばれる代理が任命され、彼らが領地の管理に当たることになった。

戦国乱世の起因の一端は守護にもあった。一四六七年、将軍継承争いに以下の小論は、徳川家康公に関する総合的な伝記ではなく、関ヶ原の合戦などの極めて重要な戦いにおける、「家康公の軍事的業績の概要」を述べることを意図している。

政治的社会的背景

一五四二年後半、日本の歴史において極めて重要な出来事が起きた。三河藩大名、松平広忠公（一五二六〜一五四九）に嫡男が誕生したのだ。

この半年後には、もうひとつの画期的な事件が九州南部沖、種子島で起こった。一五四三年八月二十五日、火縄銃を所持する三人のポルトガル人を乗せた中国の商船が嵐から避難する先を求めて種子島に漂着したのである。また、一五四二年十二月二十六日には松平広忠公に嫡男が生まれたが、当時の日本は動乱の戦国時代であった。内戦は日本の歴史全体を検証しても、さして特別なものではないが、戦国時代と呼ばれるこの時代は例外であった。領主、大名（偉大な家名）は領地をめぐり、また領地がもたらす利権や権力をめぐって争い、ほぼ一世紀の間、戦乱が続いたのである。この間、大名間の同盟関係は絶えず変わり続け、刻々と変化する戦況が自国に有利になるように編成されては解体され、そしてまた再編成されていった。しかし日本全国を平定する程の最高の権力を握るものは、未だ現れてはいなかった。過去の律令制支配とは違い、戦国時代を戦う大名はその武力拡大の為、農民を戦力に加えることに何の抵抗も持っていなかった。そして、鉄砲がポルトガル人によってもたらされ、時代に新しい要因が加わった。

鉄砲の伝来

史料によれば、鉄砲はこれより数十年前にすでに中国から伝来しており、日本人は模倣し独自の鉄砲を製造・使用したようだが、それが事実であったにせよ、歴史の流れへの大きな変化をもたらすほどの影響力はなかった。これに対し、ポルトガルから伝わった鉄砲（ポルトガルが拠点としていたインドのゴアで製造されていた鉄砲の確立が高い）は、既に、先見の明を持つ大名たちによって、その計り知れない威力が着目されていた。たしかに熟練した弓の射手は、鉄砲と同様の射程距離・命中精度を誇り、鉄砲の弾丸を補充している間に矢を一ダースほど射ることは出来たが、弓を的確に射るに為には何年もの訓練が必要とされた。一方、鉄砲を持った足軽は、ほんの数日の訓練によって、最も訓練された武士と対等に戦うことが出来たからである。鉄砲の普及はそれまでの戦闘方法に新しい機軸が求められることとなり、弓矢や刀剣などの伝統的な武器の訓練を積んだ武士は、新しく高価な武器を所持した足軽鉄砲隊の援護に回るということになった。

大名が武力増強のために注文するにつれて、鉄砲の製造は数年ほどで、堺、国友などの地方で主要産業となっていった。鉄砲伝来からわずか六年後（一五四九）、大名織田信秀は国友で鉄砲五百丁を注文した。また二十年後には、大名が何千丁もの鉄砲で武装することは当たり前のことになっていった。豊臣秀吉（一五三七〜一五九八）による天下統一後、鉄砲による武装が抑えられたにもかかわらず、一六〇〇年の時点で、二十万丁の鉄砲が日本に存在していたと言われている。十六世紀の後半、日本は世界で最大の鉄砲製造国および使用国となっていた。

最初にやってきたポルトガル人の貿易商たちに続いて、イエズス会の宣教師が渡来し、キリスト教への布教を熱心に説いた。日本と明朝（中国）間にあった外交上の緊張関係に、ポルトガル人が乗じる期間は長くは続かなかった。生絹と中国の錦織物への大きな需要が日本に生じ、この需要は倭寇などの形でのみ供給されていた。まもなくポルトガル船はマカオの中国人と取引するため、繊維・象牙・ワインなどを積んで、ゴアから出航した。ゴアでポルトガル人は、日本へ輸出する生絹・錦織物・その他の贅沢品を積み込み、日本からは銀などをヨーロッパに輸出した。

ポルトガル人の渡来と鉄砲の伝来が、権力と領土をめぐって争い続ける大名たちに、直接的に大きな影響を与えた訳ではなかった。三河藩の大名松平家は、強大な力を持つ二つの隣国にはさまれ、しばしばその侵略を受けた。鉄砲を積極的に入手した尾張の大名織田信秀、もう一方は駿河の今川義元（一五一九〜一五六〇）であった。一五四七年、広忠公の叔父松平信孝は、松平家の実権をめぐって広忠公を攻撃した。また刈谷の水野信元（広

ROYAL ARMOURIES

Armouries Drive
Leeds
Yorkshire LS10 1LT
Telephone 0113 220 1999

ロイヤル・アーマリーズへ、そして特別展「将軍：徳川家康公の生涯」へ皆様をお迎えできることをたいへん嬉しく存じます。

本特別展は、世界遺産に指定される日光東照宮とロイヤル・アーマリーズの13年間に及ぶパートナーシップのハイライトとなる記念すべきイベントです。日英間の国家的・文化的な繋がりは強く、実際400年以上前に徳川将軍が英国国王ジェームス一世に甲冑一式を贈呈した頃まで遡ることができます。その甲冑も、今回披露される目を瞠る数々の展示物の一部に含まれています。

日本国外で初めて一堂に会すこれらの貴重な品々をロイヤル・アーマリーズに託していただけたことはたいへん栄誉なことです。企画にあたっては多大な時間とエネルギーが注がれており、その成功はひとえに英国および日本の数多くの研究機関および個人の方々からいただいたご教示と技術、熱意と惜しまぬ努力に負っています。ここですべてのお名前を挙げて謝意を表することはできませんが、日光東照宮の稲葉久雄宮司には特に心からお礼を申し上げたいと思います。稲葉氏の個人的なご配慮、そして日光東照宮関係者すべてのご支援がなかったならば、本展覧会は実現しなかったことでしょう。

今回の特別展は、世界各地の武器・甲冑とその歴史を多く人に興味深く教育的なものとなるよう献身しているロイヤル・アーマリーズの持続的な努力の一端です。本特別展および関連アクティビティを楽しんでいただけますこと、またこのカタログが今回のご訪問と日本で最も有名な将軍、徳川家康について思い出す記念となることを願っております。

ロイヤル・アーマリーズ、チェアマン
アン・M・グリーン

NIKKO TOSHOGU SHRINE

ごあいさつ

日光東照宮
宮司　稲 葉 久 雄

1991年にロイヤル・アーマリーズと当宮が姉妹施設の締結をしてから14年を数えます。この間、宝物の相互交換展示、当宮流鏑馬の英国公演や英国中世武術団による日光公演の実施などの交流事業を重ね、着実に関係を深めて参りました。

このたび、これらの交流事業がひとつの結実を見ることとなり、予てより計画されておりました共催による特別展「将軍：徳川家康公の生涯」が開催できますことはこの上ない喜びであります。

わが徳川家康公は、戦国騒乱の世に生を享け、幾多の艱難を克服し、天下統一の偉業を成し遂げられ、世界の歴史に比類なき江戸時代260年の太平をもたらし、近代日本発展への礎を築かれた不世出の英傑であります。当宮と致しましては、この特別展に英国民の皆様をはじめ他国よりも大勢の方々が観覧に訪れ、公の偉大な御事績が広く認識されることを期待しております。

終わりに、本展開催にあたり、快くレセプション会場をご提供下さったヘアウッド卿をはじめ、展覧会会場となるロイヤル・アーマリーズ、リーズ館の関係各位、資料出品に際し、特段のご協力を賜りました各館関係各位に対し、衷心より御礼申し上げます。

稲葉久雄

2301 Sannai Nikko, Tochigi
Telephone: 0288-54-0560

将軍
徳川家康公の生涯